# REVOLUTION
IN THE
# CHURCH

# REVOLUTION
### IN THE
# CHURCH

CHALLENGING THE RELIGIOUS SYSTEM
WITH A CALL FOR RADICAL CHANGE

## Michael L. Brown

**Chosen Books**
A Division of Baker Book House Co
Grand Rapids, Michigan 49516

Published by Chosen Books
a division of Baker Book House Company
P.O. Box 6287, Grand Rapids, MI 49516-6287

Printed in the United States of America

**Library of Congress Cataloging-in-Publication Data**

Brown, Michael L., 1955–
    Revolution in the church : challenging the religious system with a call for radical change / Michael L. Brown.
        p.    cm.
    Includes bibliographical references and index.
    ISBN 0-8007-9310-2 (pbk.)
    1. Church renewal. I. Title.
BV600 .B8515 2002
262′ .001′7—dc21                     2002004704

For current information about all releases from Baker Book House, visit our web site:
               http://www.bakerbooks.com

# Contents

Contents

# Preface

On February 14, 2001, the leadership team for FIRE School of Ministry in Pensacola, Florida, was meeting with Derek Brown, a dear fellow worker from England. As we were talking with Derek about our vision to see the Jesus revolution make an impact on our society, he made a simple but profound comment: "Before there can be a revolution in the society, there must first be a revolution in the Church."

Of course! There must first be radical, change within the Body before we can bring radical change to the world. Derek's comment stayed with me, ultimately leading to the writing of this book. But not a single word was written as an exercise in abstract theology. The pages that follow reflect years of wrestling through the issue of what really constitutes the New Testament norm for "the Church."

More importantly, these pages reflect the importance of actually living out these scriptural truths. *That* is where one is constantly reminded that talk is cheap, especially with the younger generation—a generation that desperately wants reality, not hype. Not only must revolution be a subject of discussion; it must also be a subject of action.

Please take this book as my personal invitation to come along on the journey being undertaken by multitudes of believers across the world.

I hope you will find practical answers in these chapters, along with some fresh new challenges, since all of us at one time or another have probably done our part to promote what I refer to as "the religious system," which exists wherever human ways take precedence over divine ways; wherever the will and wisdom of man are superimposed over the will and wisdom of God; wherever church traditions become more sacred than the clear teaching of God's Word; wherever spiritual progress is thwarted by the flesh, however "religious" that flesh might appear to be.

I only urge caution to all who would challenge this system. It is costly and treacherous to go against the grain, since the moment we imagine ourselves to be God's elite, last-days remnant, we have fallen into spiritual pride, which itself is an insidious part of the system we desire to change. Let us proceed with humility, then, asking the Lord to search *our* hearts first, to strip us of all religious pretension and to deliver us from bondage to dead tradition. Let the revolution begin with us!

My appreciation to Jane Campbell of Chosen Books (she is the living embodiment of the word *editor*), for wholeheartedly embracing this project and pursuing its completion with excellence and enthusiasm. Thanks are also due to project editor Kristin Kornoelje for helping to ensure the quality of the work.

My profound thanks to the courageous FIRE community—the leadership team, faculty and staff, the incredible army of students and grads, and to our community as a whole. The best is yet to come! Bless you all for not losing the vision. Bless you for believing the dream. And to Nancy, the joy of my life and my precious bride of more than 26 years—I would not have made it this far without you.

On with the revolution! Jesus, lead the way!

# 1

# A Dog Food Revolution?

---

SOME REVEALING SIGNS OF THE TIMES

---

Revolution is one of the looser words. The great French Revolution, the American Revolution, the Industrial Revolution, a revolution in Haiti, a social revolution, the American Negro Revolution, a revolution in our thinking, or in the ladies' garment trade, or in the automotive industry—the list could be almost endless.

Crane Brinton, *The Anatomy of Revolution*
(first edition published 1938)

If all possible meanings of the term "revolution" were to be encompassed within a short definition, then perhaps three words would suffice: "sweeping dramatic change."

Jaroslav Krej, *Great Revolutions Compared*

> We must become the change we envision.
>
> Mahatma Gandhi, quoted in
> *Revolution: Faces of Change*

> Join the ®evolution.
>
> RadioShack Corporation,
> 2000 Annual Report, front cover

The ad was striking, taking up the entire back page of the sports section of *USA Today,* June 26, 2000. A major company had made some exciting new changes, changes so bold and radical only one word could adequately describe the enormity of it all. That word ran the entire width of the page and was printed in four colors: blue, yellow, red and green. That word, of course, was *revolution.* A Zest soap revolution! A revolution in the shower! That is exactly how the ad expressed it:

> Four new colors & fragrances. Twice the lather of soap. Twice the fun. It's a refreshingly different kind of clean.
> NEW ZEST BODY WASH. ZESTFULLY CLEAN. REFRESHINGLY DIFFERENT.

A body wash revolution? But this is a sign of the times. Revolution is everywhere, and everything is revolutionary. There is a mattress revolution—a whole new way to sleep—and a groundbreaking Revolution protein bar, not to mention the inventive Revolution hosta plant for your garden.

Even more daring and trend-setting is the innovative dog food brand named Revolution. Yes, it is true. Today your pooch can munch on Revolution dog food while you dine on Revolution protein bars. And when you lose interest in the protein bars, you can cook up your favorite cuisine in the Revolution line of pots and pans!

The good news does not end there. If your dog ends up getting heartworms, you can give him a dose of selamectin—better known as Revolution—"a newer topical insecticide, wormer and heartworm preventative."[1] The revolution continues.

We are in the grip of a technology revolution, a PC revolution, a wireless revolution, a banking revolution, a cell phone revolution, a learning revolution, an e-book revolution and even a childless revolution.[2] And there are endless sports revolutions, including tennis racket revolutions, baseball bat revolutions, and a new line of Revolution golf balls and golf clubs, with a matching Revolution cap. You can even build your own Revolution bike.[3]

If that bores you, check out the Game Revolution web site (www.game-revolution.com) with all programming and content copyrighted by Net Revolution, Inc., or, if movies are your thing, you can watch something new from Revolution Studios in Hollywood, producing the latest in cutting-edge cinematography. E-commerce is also making its mark, as an Internet article exclaimed, "From Retail to E-tail: It's a Revolution."[4] This is a time of large-scale paradigm shifts!

In the business sector in particular, revolutionary terminology is rampant. Best-selling books published in the year 2000 alone include Guy Kawasaki's *Rules for Revolutionaries: The Capitalist Manifesto for Creating and Marketing New Products and Services* and Gary Hamel's *Leading the Revolution,* a volume with a very focused plan of attack: I. Facing Up to the Revolution; II. Finding the Revolution; III. Igniting the Revolution; IV. Sustaining the Revolution. (Remember that he is speaking of a *business* revolution.)[5]

The handwriting is on the wall. This is a season of wide-scale, radical change, even if the word *revolution* is being overused. But it is being overused for a reason: These are revolutionary times.

Consider the striking results of a business survey cited by Christian author Leonard Sweet: "A poll of business executives found an astonishing 49 percent taking the most radical position they could take about the future: we are living in revolutionary times and are at the very beginnings of an entirely new economic era that requires a fundamental revolution of how we live, work, and play."[6]

The Church world is also marked by a growing revolutionary mentality. The new Jesus Revolution is a major theme of The Call events, beginning with The Call D.C. on September 2, 2000, when more than 300,000 believers—primarily young people—gathered for a day of fasting and prayer at the foot of the U.S. Capitol. More and more books and articles call for some kind of spiritual revolution,[7] while an increasing number of songs proclaim the theme as well.[8] All this reflects the consensus that this generation has fallen so far that only a spiritual and moral revolution can turn things around.[9]

Yet before there can be a revolution in the world, there must first be a revolution in the Church. *That* is where everything must start.

For many, however, the thought of revolution in the Church is unsettling. What if some of our spiritual foundations need adjusting? What if sweeping, even extreme, change is required? What if our very concept of "church" must be overhauled? What if it costs some of us our jobs, our livelihoods, our careers?

*Revolution,* rightly understood, is a disturbing word. Simply stated, there is no such thing as a nice revolution. Or, to express it another way: A revolution that costs nothing is worth nothing. How revolutionary do you really want to be?

12

For years now we have bemoaned the state of the Western Church, longing for change, praying for revival, looking for new methods and programs and ideas. And God has answered us in many wonderful ways; some real progress has been made. But I fear that most of us have not yet realized how serious the problem is and have failed, therefore, to realize just how serious—how sweeping and wide-ranging and dramatic and radical—the solution must be.

There is a reason why thousands of churches close down every year in America. There is a reason cities with thousands of church buildings—some of them packed out on Sunday mornings—are hardly affected by those churches. There is a reason our airwaves are flooded with Gospel TV and Gospel radio, yet Hollywood rules the day. There is a reason why church growth in America has stagnated for more than two decades. There is a reason, but do we really want to hear it?

According to Martin Luther, "The most permanent fate of God's word is that for its sake the world is put into uproar. For the sermon of God comes in order to change and revive the whole earth to the extent that it reaches it." Or, as explained by Professor Hannah Arendt, "the 'revolution' which, according to Luther, shakes the world when the Word of God is liberated from the traditional authority of the Church is constant and applies to all forms of secular government; it does not establish a new secular order but constantly and permanently shakes the foundations of all worldly establishment."[10] Yet we see nothing even faintly resembling the revolutionary power of the Word in our culture. Something is terribly wrong.

Go to any city in America and you will find that the Mormons work together and the Jehovah's Witnesses work together, but that the Christians cannot even agree on who among them is really on the same team. Why?

In New Testament days each city had one church, meeting in many different locations—just as each city today has one Catholic church, with numerous parishes. But getting even one-tenth of the leaders of the Protestant churches in a city to pray together one time is considered a major accomplishment. This should not be!

And how do we explain the conspicuous absence of divine power in our midst if, as many of us believe, the gifts and power of the Holy Spirit, including divine healing, continue to this day? Yet after almost one hundred years of "Pentecostal" outpouring, we are still trying to figure out how to see the sick healed on a consistent basis. Something is not lining up. Could it be that we need a revolution?

Andy Law, co-founder and chairman of the British advertising firm St. Luke's, told the incredible story of his company's overnight rise to prominence in his 1998 book *Open Minds: 21ˢᵗ Century Business Lessons and Innovations from St. Luke's*.[11] The volume begins with "Ten Ways to Create a Revolution in Your Company," calling for some extremely unsettling steps:

1. Ask yourself what you want out of life.
2. Ask yourself what really matters to you.
3. Give all your work clothes to Oxfam and wear what you feel is really you.
4. Talk to people (even those you don't like) about 1 and 2. (You should be feeling very uncomfortable now. You may even be sick. This is normal.)
5. Give up something you most need at work (desk, company car, etc.).
6. Trust everyone you meet. Keep every agreement you make. (You should be feeling better now.)
7. Undergo a group experience (anything goes—parachuting, holidaying).

8. Rewrite your business plan to align all the above with your customers.
9. Draw a line on the office floor and invite everyone to a brave new world.
10. Share everything you do and own fairly with everyone who crosses the line. (You should be feeling liberated. Soon you will have, in this order, the following: grateful customers, inspired employees, friendly communities, money.)[12]

This is precisely what Andy Law and St. Luke's did, with no employees having their own desks or PCs. (Everything is shared by everyone, and the company is run along the lines of a cell group church—although it is a secular, not Christian, company.) Radical steps produced radical results, starting a business revolution.

Yet I fear that, once again, the words of Jesus apply, and we can see that "the people of this world are more shrewd in dealing with their own kind than are the people of the light" (Luke 16:8). Worldly people understand just how extreme and costly true revolution is—even in business—while we, the people of God, prefer to sing about revolution and preach about revolution and write about revolution and even pray about revolution rather than take revolutionary action and make revolutionary choices.

Who wants *that* kind of revolution in the Church—a revolution that challenges our traditional styles and structures, questions our traditional methods and models, and confronts our traditional forms and fetishes (we have fetishes in the Church too!)? Who wants *that* kind of revolution?

Just imagine what would happen if we actually took Jesus or Paul at face value and began to do what they said. It truly would be revolutionary. Yet a veil seems to cover our eyes when we read the Scriptures. How else

15

do we explain the fact that we can read Jesus' words in Luke 14:12–14 many times over without being struck by the fact that we should actually do what He commanded? Yet the meaning of the Lord's words is perfectly clear. Here are the verses once again:

> "When you give a luncheon or dinner, do not invite your friends, your brothers or relatives, or your rich neighbors; if you do, they may invite you back and so you will be repaid. But when you give a banquet, invite the poor, the crippled, the lame, the blind, and you will be blessed. Although they cannot repay you, you will be repaid at the resurrection of the righteous."

What do we know about *this kind* of banquet?

Or consider the example of Paul. Many leaders today have rightly argued that the New Testament teaches there are apostles in the Church today. That alone is quite a revolutionary concept for some. Yet a number of Paul's most important statements about apostolic ministry have been completely overlooked. Why is it that we quote one verse while ignoring another? The chief of the apostles wrote:

> It seems to me that God has put us apostles on display at the end of the procession, like men condemned to die in the arena. We have been made a spectacle to the whole universe, to angels as well as to men. We are fools for Christ, but you are so wise in Christ! We are weak, but you are strong! You are honored, we are dishonored! To this very hour we go hungry and thirsty, we are in rags, we are brutally treated, we are homeless. We work hard with our own hands. When we are cursed, we bless; when we are persecuted, we endure it; when we are slandered, we answer kindly. Up to this moment we have become the scum of the earth, the refuse of the world.
>
> 1 Corinthians 4:9–13

Who wants to be *that* kind of apostle? We love the beginning of the procession, not the end. We find our identity in a flashy TV spectacle before the viewing audience, not a mocking, painful spectacle before the whole universe. How revolutionary do we want to be?[13]

Will we be revolutionaries for Jesus if it means the loss of titles and prestige and power?

Will we be revolutionaries for Jesus if it means the loss of friends and family?

Will we be revolutionaries for Jesus if it means the loss of money?

Will we be revolutionaries for Jesus if it means misunderstanding and even expulsion?

Will we be revolutionaries for Jesus if it means we question the purpose of our multimillion-dollar church building used a precious few hours a week?

Will we be revolutionaries for Jesus if it means massive personal upheaval?

Will we? Will you?

A growing army of holy radicals is saying *Yes!* to all the above. Their example should give you courage and faith to take a bold, even militant new stand. Their example should give you strength to get out of the boat and walk on the water toward Jesus. Their example should inspire you to fly.

In reality, we have no other choice. It is revolution or bust, revolution or we die, revolution or . . . I would rather not fill in the blank! Let's just start a revolution—in the Church, where it belongs. From there we can change the world.

# 2

# It's Time to Wake Up!

## WE CANNOT AFFORD TO SLEEP OUR WAY
## THROUGH ANOTHER REVOLUTION

If the Lord tarries, young men now preparing for the ministry will be preaching for at least twenty years in the most complex revolutionary period that has been seen in modern times. This revolution is not like the many political upsets of Europe and South America. Today's arising is world revolution.

William Ward Ayer,
"Preaching to Combat the Present Revolution"
*Bibliotheca Sacra* (July 1967)

We live in the most revolutionary period of human history. . . . Social band-aids and reform antiseptics give little hope for a cure or even an improvement. A revolution is needed.... You can experience this revolution. In fact, you can help bring it to pass.

Bill Bright, *Revolution Now!* (1969)

I'm convinced America is at her crisis hour. *Revolution is inevitable.* It's just a matter of which faction is going to prove strongest and will win out in the end. I believe most Americans are so apathetic that they will just sit back and go to whoever wins the struggle.

Tom Skinner, *Words of Revolution* (1970)

Day after day men came to help David, until he had a great army, like the army of God. These are the numbers of the men armed for battle who came to David at Hebron to turn Saul's kingdom over to him, as the LORD had said ... *men of Issachar, who understood the times and knew what Israel should do*—200 chiefs, with all their relatives under their command.

1 Chronicles 12:22–23, 32, emphasis added

What used to be considered morally reprehensible is now recommended as a positive value; what was once called demoralization is now styled moral progress and a new freedom.

Pitirim Sorokin, *The American Sex Revolution* (1956)

We'll get you through your children.

Allen Ginsberg (1958)

America experienced a cultural revolution in the 1960s, and the effects of that revolution have been felt into the new millennium. As Roger Kimball observed:

The Age of Aquarius did not end when the last electric guitar was unplugged at Woodstock. It lives on in our values and habits, in our tastes, pleasures, and aspira-

19

tions. It lives on especially in our educational and cultural institutions, and in the degraded pop culture that permeates our lives like a corrosive fog. . . . Although sometimes tempted to ignore it, we are living in the aftermath of a momentous social and moral assault.[1]

To buttress his position, Kimball called several other authors to testify to the great changes that took place in our nation from the 1960s right on into the '70s:

* According to David Frum, we are the heirs of "the most total social transformation that the United States has lived through since the coming of industrialism, a transformation (a revolution!) that has not ended yet."[2]
* Philosopher Paul Oskar Kristeller, writing in 1991, stated, "We have witnessed what amounts to a cultural revolution, comparable to the one in China if not worse, and whereas the Chinese have to some extent overcome their cultural revolution, I see many signs that ours is getting worse all the time, and no indication that it will be overcome in the foreseeable future."[3]
* Judge Robert Bork, in his important work *Slouching Towards Gomorrah,* claimed that "the Sixties may be seen in the universities as a mini-French Revolution that seemed to fail but did not. The radicals were not defeated by a conservative or traditionally liberal opposition but by their own graduation from the universities. And theirs was merely a temporary defeat. They and their ideology are all around us now."[4]

What this means in practical terms is that our public school teachers can hand out condoms but not Gospel

20

tracts; that homosexuals have more right to freedom of expression in the classroom than do evangelical Christians; that churches have to encourage *believing teenagers* to remain virgins until marriage; that by the mid-1990s the majority of women giving birth to their firstborn children conceived those children out of wedlock; that we have moved from *Leave It to Beaver* to *Melrose Place* and from Mike Douglas (do you remember his daily TV talk show?) to Jerry Springer. That is just the tip of the iceberg.

I have conducted impromptu surveys while speaking throughout America, asking all those fifty years old or more to stand up and respond to two questions: First, "When you were in high school, did you know of anyone your age who either tried to commit suicide or actually committed suicide?" Invariably just a few hands go up (in some cases, not one hand is raised). Second, "When you were in high school, did you know of any girls your age who either had a child out of wedlock or had an abortion?" In this case, a few more hands go up, but it is still a small portion of those standing.

I then repeat this with young people between the ages of fifteen and nineteen. Without fail, when I put the same questions to them, almost every hand is raised in response (many times, every single hand is raised). And many of these kids are "church kids" educated in Christian schools or even home-schooled. What a different world they are being raised in, and what a changed society confronts them at every turn in life—yet this is the only society they have ever known.

What makes my unofficial survey all the more striking is that the few in the older crowd who raised their hands did so because they knew of *one person* in their entire school who fit the description, whereas many of the teens know of *numerous people* who fit the description. A revolution did make an impact on our society one generation ago, and the results of it are undeniable. The year 1968 in particular was a turning point, not only in America, but also around the globe.

It was in 1968 that Dr. Martin Luther King Jr. and Robert F. Kennedy were assassinated. Hippie and yippie activists rocked Chicago during the Democratic convention. Bloody riots broke out in inner cities and student protests erupted on college campuses, often producing dramatic change. In fact, at the beginning of 1968 some secular universities had curfews and dress codes. By the end of the year those rules were gone, a thing of the past, almost unthinkable in today's society.

One of my friends living in Israel today, a Jewish believer saved in the early 1970s, told me that when he first attended college in the fall of 1967, almost all the young men were in fraternities and hardly any of them had long hair or took drugs. One year later, in the fall of 1968, things had changed dramatically. Everywhere he looked, young men were growing their hair long, doing drugs and dropping out of fraternities. What a change one year had wrought!

A pastor who grew up in small-town America told me that he and his teenage friends used to hang out together and get drunk. Then, he said, it seemed as if over the course of one week in 1969 (it took a little longer for the cultural changes to hit small towns), all his friends stopped getting drunk and started getting high. As Bob Dylan sang, "The times they are a-changin'."

In France the May Revolution of 1968 began on college campuses and spread to twelve million workers throughout the nation, almost toppling the government of Charles de Gaulle. Similar tremors rocked the rest of Europe—so much so that the generation in Germany shaped by those events is called "the 1968 generation."[5] In Mexico, too, home to the 1968 Olympics (remembered for the defiant Black Power gesture made on the winning platform by three black American athletes), college campuses erupted in nonviolent protests, joined by the populace at large. The government stopped the protests forcibly, culminating in the Tlalteloco Massacre of October 2, in which hundreds of parents, students and children were gunned down. As one Mexican translator told me, "After that, everything went downhill in our country." Or, from a more studied perspective, "Relations between Mexican citizens and their government were to be marred by an air of cynicism from that point on."[6]

Yes, the 1960s and early '70s were years of tremendous upheaval and change, years of shaking and disruption, years of moral and cultural revolution. Yet for the most part the Church slept her way through the revolution. The devil seized the moment while God's people missed the opportunity of a century. What on earth were we doing?

Speaking of the sexual revolution, a 1982 article in *Esquire* magazine observed:

> The revolution enjoyed one swift victory after another. Filmed and printed erotica that would have shocked in 1965 elicited yawns in 1975. Within less than a decade, the sexual experiments of West Coast college students and hippies became the stuff of every day life for blue-collar workers in Des Moines and Texarkana. Perhaps never before had such a radical shift in mores occurred in so short a time.[7]

In light of this fleshly onslaught, Randy Alcorn, author of the probing book *Christians in the Wake of the Sexual Revolution,* could only ask, "Where was the church when all this was happening? What did it do to counter the country's moral decline?"[8] His carefully documented answer is a painful pill to swallow: For the

23

most part, American Christians did not counter the country's moral decline; we contributed to it. We participated in it. The darkness made the light dimmer rather than the light exposing and brightening the darkness. What an indictment![9]

Another indictment is even more painful to recognize: The Church missed one of the greatest potential spiritual harvests in modern history, since the 1960s were a time of seeking and questioning, a time when the very meaning of life was up for grabs, when the gods of materialism and greed were renounced and the power of dead traditionalism was cast off. What a golden opportunity for the people of God to rise up and say, "We have the answer! We have the real thing!" But we missed the moment. To this hour, the thought of it causes me pain. How many lives were needlessly destroyed?

It seems that even *Mad* magazine had more spiritual insight into those critical years than did many Christian leaders, satirizing the late 1960s as a time of great spiritual hunger, especially among young people. The April 1968 edition of *Mad* featured Alfred E. Newman on the cover, pictured as a hippie surrounded by the words "Turn On, Tune In, Drop Dead." True to form, this particular issue contained a mock new periodical called *Hippie, The Magazine That Turns You On*. *Hippie* was acutely aware of the signs of the times.

Among the headline articles was "What to Do About God After You Finally Find Him," while *Hippie*'s classified ads included: "Young Male Hippie, leaving for India to find God, desires Young Female Traveling Companion in case I don't connect"; and, "Looking For God? I will tell you where to find Him. No kidding, I know where He's at, and who He is. $1.00 gets this information. Your money back in 7 days if you're not completely satisfied with Him."[10] Other ads pointed to Eastern spirituality, including mountains for both meditation and

24

sexual adventures along with cures for hernias by sitting in the lotus position. How accurately this parodied the spiritual journey so many young people were on.

*Mad* even had the insight to recognize how many Jewish seekers populated that 1968 generation, creating hippie names such as Mohammad Tishman, Zen Rappaport and Shah Bernbaum, and featuring a counseling column by "Abba Bennadam" (Hebrew for *Father, Son of Man*), a "Mystic, a Seer, a Prophet, a Poet, a Free-Thinker and an Aluminum Storm Door Salesman" (the latter, of course, to provide an income!). One of the questions posed to him came from "Rattled," living in Chicago: "Dear Abba: I am approaching 30, and I still haven't found God! Man, I'm getting uptight over it! How and where can I find Him?" Abba replied, "*Dear Rattled: Don't lose your cool. I'll tell Him you're looking for Him the next time I see Him.*"

Do you grasp the significance of all this? The spiritual search of these young people was so obvious that *Mad* could satirize it in the silliest terms. Yet God's people hardly recognized how ripe these radical seekers were, failing to present them with a radical Jesus—the Jesus of the New Testament rather than the Jesus of the traditional church. In just a few short pages, *Mad* made reference to hippies trying to "find God" four separate times, yet those who knew Him did precious little to make Him known.

To say it once more: We failed to seize the opportunity of a lifetime during the lifetime of the opportunity.[11] We miserably missed the moment. But Satan did not miss the moment. He rushed in to fill the void with sexual freedom, illicit drugs, rock music and its message of rebellion, Transcendental Meditation and Eastern religions, and every kind of activist cause, from the admirable to the absurd. What a harvest hell reaped! Again I ask, What were God's people doing?

Perhaps the excitement of the charismatic renewal of the 1960s diverted our attention. Perhaps it was sufficient for us to express outrage over the degeneration of society. (After all, isn't that a large part of our calling—standing stiffly in our stained-glass sanctuaries and denouncing the sins of the world?) Perhaps the momentous events of the Six-Day War in 1967, returning the Old City of Jerusalem to Jewish control, signaled the end of the age and the soon return of the Messiah, contributing to a theology of escapism and defeat:[12] "Why even try to resist the downward trend in society, since everything is only going to get worse from here on anyway?"

A review of my book *Revolution! The Call to Holy War*, posted on the Internet, gives some insight into this way of thinking. The reviewer, no doubt a sincere and well-meaning Christian leader, responded to a request from someone who sent him a copy of *Revolution!*, asking for his thoughts. He did find some value in what I wrote, but his conclusion was decidedly negative because, in his view, it is too late for change in our society. He explained:

> The main premise of the book is, in the author's words, "a call to spark the most sweeping counterculture movement in our nation's history," in short, to change our society through religious revival. Is this God's message? Is this on His agenda?
>
> There are two distinct periods in history that are, I believe, direct parallels of our day: Noah's day; and the period of time from Christ's earthly ministry until the destruction of Jerusalem. In both cases, judgment was looming. In neither case was there any suggestion from God that the fundamental situation could be altered. In both cases a way of escape was provided and the truth was preached for the benefit of any who had ears to hear. God's people were delivered. The rest perished.

26

Why did Noah not preach revival, or revolution? Why did Jesus and the apostles not preach them? BECAUSE THAT WAS NOT GOD'S MESSAGE! . . . Why wasn't revival and reformation preached? Because it wasn't God's message. It was past time for those things. Judgment was inevitable. God was in the business of rescuing His elect from the general destruction. . . .

Our job is to wait on God and be in harmony with what He is saying and doing in the earth. We can't manufacture revival or revolution if God isn't in it! . . .[13]

So the window is closed, and there will be *no* worldwide outpouring, *no* worldwide revival, *no* widespread reformation, *no* widespread Jesus revolution. All we can do is warn sinners about the coming wrath and prepare ourselves to meet God.

Yet the reviewer does not totally reject the concept of revival, noting that

We ourselves, here in Southern Pines, North Carolina, experienced a great move of God in the late '60s. I'm thankful for it but we don't try to perpetuate it or preach that some of its more unusual aspects should be sought out as the "norm." For example, angels visited us—with a specific message regarding the loosing of Satan and the soon return of Christ.

These believers claim they experienced a revival *in the late 1960s,* replete with angelic visitations and a special message for the hour: "The end is near! Jesus is about to return and Satan is about to be loosed to lead the world into rebellion against God (see Revelation 20:7–10)—and it's all going downhill from here."

Not so! That is not the message of the Scriptures, nor do I believe that is what the Holy Spirit is saying today, regardless of whether these were true angelic visitations, regardless of whether this was a bona fide revival, and regardless of whether God was speaking to His people through these messages. The interpretation of the messages was dead wrong, since the Word does not teach that the Great Commission of Jesus *decreases* in scope at the end of the age. Rather, it *increases* (see Matthew 13:39: "The harvest is the end of the age"; Matthew 24:14; Revelation 7:9–10). The authority Jesus received and the authority with which He sends us is *to the ends of the earth until the end of the age* (see Matthew 28:18–20). In fact, more people were saved worldwide in the last thirty years of the last century than in any hundred-year period of Church history before (and this is an understatement).[14]

How sad, then, that another reader of *Revolution!*— the one who supplied the reviewer with a copy—could say, "To me the book portrayed a Pied Piper luring youngsters into his fantasy."[15]

> Unfortunately many gullible & innocent people fall for this kind of thing. Wrap something with the Name of Christ & people jump on the bandwagon because there is no discernment. I have been hearing about "revival" non-stop for years now, but have been seeing a great falling away instead. It has come to me that even though there is a church on every corner this country has become morally unraveled. A large percentage of people, when polled, profess to be Christian yet we have rampant decline. How can that be, I asked myself?
>
> For some time now I have held the unpopular opinion that we are about to experience the judgment of God. I personally feel we have passed the point of no return.[16]

Tragically, this theology of defeat produces a mentality of retreat, and this was exactly what happened in the 1960s. For one reason or another, God's people slept their way through a massive cultural revolution and missed an opportunity to provide reality to a confused and disillusioned generation.

Others, however, were not asleep. Speaking of the turning point in modern homosexual history, the Stonewall riots in New York City in 1969, gay activist Mark Rubin asks, "How did that singular event in June 1969 become the fountainhead for so many of the changes that have made the world so different for queers thirty years later?" His answer? "It spawned the Gay Liberation Movement."[17]

> First there was The Gay Liberation Front proclaiming loudly, clearly, and brilliantly, the truth that gay is good, that queers had embodied within them all of the genius of Humanity, and owned all privileges of that status. . . .

> GLF, the Gay Liberation Front, was conceived as being part of the entire Liberation movement, one segment of a worldwide struggle against oppression. . . .

> The Gay Activists Alliance stood for writing the revolution into law. Although individual members would ally themselves with causes not directly related to the oppression of homosexuals, the organization's single issue focus enabled it [sic] direct all of its energies toward working intensively in, on, with, and against "The Establishment" on issues effecting [sic] lesbians and gay men.

> It said, "We demand our Liberation *from* repression and *to* the point where repressive laws are removed from the books and our rights are written into the documents that protect the rights of all people, for without that writing there can be no guarantees of protection from the larger society."

> The means to achieving these ends included, street actions famously defined as "zaps", marches, picket

lines, political lobbying, education, active promotion of the need for lesbians and gay men to come out of their closets, and a constant in-your-face presentation of the fact that gay is good. Its goals were revolutionary in that it sought, through these means, to restructure society.[18]

The homosexual activists were not only unashamed; they pursued an agenda *to change society*—and they succeeded. Today there is even a gay pride month in Israel.

God's people missed their opportunity, but gay and lesbian activists did not miss theirs. And while we were trying to overcome our shame and convince ourselves to stand up and be counted, groups like STAR, the Street Transvestite Activist Revolution, made themselves heard.[19] For this we should feel ashamed. Without a Bible to guide them, without a Holy Spirit to lead them, without eternal life to encourage them, homosexuals birthed and carried forth an ambitious agenda that changed an entire generation. Whatever became of our agenda?

Of course, there *were* Christian voices in the late 1960s recognizing the nature of the hour and proclaiming Jesus as the greatest revolutionary ever.[20] But these voices were few and far between. And while, in some cases, they adequately diagnosed the gravity of the situation, most of them failed to prescribe an equally serious solution. We failed to fight fire with fire. We failed to realize that the best answer to a sexual revolution is a spiritual revolution; that the best answer to homosexual activism is Holy Spirit activism; that the best answer to women's liberation is liberation into the fullness of womanhood through the Gospel. And we failed to realize that where a revolution was needed most was within the Church itself—another fact painfully illustrated in those turbulent years when God rose up and began to move in what has become known as the Jesus People Movement or the Jesus Revolution.[21]

Yes, the Jesus People Movement was a bona fide work of the Spirit, bringing tens of thousands of hippies and rebels into the kingdom. From 1970 until 1975, in particular, radically lost young people became radically saved. (I was one of them!)[22] Rock musicians high on drugs had genuine visions of Jesus and quit getting high. Student activists came under divine conviction and, in tears, surrendered their lives to the Lord. Long-haired, guru-following, bead-wearing spiritual seekers came into traditional churches in droves.

One young Italian man, seeking spiritual enlightenment in India, met another young man looking for God. They decided to walk and hitchhike from India to Jerusalem, somehow believing they would find God there. And they did! That man is now a dear friend, having served as an evangelist and missionary in his homeland of Italy for more than 25 years.

A Korean colleague's testimony is even more dramatic. Raised in a Christian home, he concluded that the organized Church had failed and that the only way to truly implement the teachings of Jesus was through Marxism. He was the leader of the student activists at Seoul University—the most prestigious school in the country—and had gathered signatures on petitions calling for the resignation of the president, whom the activists blamed for all the country's problems. In fact, he was scheduled to meet with the president and present the petitions—actually sitting in a waiting room before his appointment—when a pastor who had known him since his childhood happened to meet him there. It was a divine appointment.

The pastor turned to this young zealot and asked him, "Has it ever occurred to you that the problems in Korea are *your* fault?" Those words went right through him, and suddenly this confident student leader fell to the floor in tears, then stood to his feet a new man, promptly launching a Gospel ministry on the university campus. I have preached for him many times, addressing some of the Christian leaders he has helped to train at campuses in South Korea. The year of his conversion (and mine, too) was 1971, when the Jesus People Movement was in full gear.

The fruit is undeniable: Most of the Jewish believers I know today who are in full-time ministry were saved as hippies between 1970 and 1975, and many of the American missionaries now serving in other countries came to the Lord as hippies during the same time.

That is the glorious part of the story. The tragic, even pathetic, part of the story is this: For the most part, the Church slept through this revolution, too. God Almighty took decisive action, bringing myriads of sinners to the very doors of our church buildings, and we *still* did not understand what was happening. We *still* went on with business as usual, not providing new wineskins for the new wine, not understanding how to disciple this radical young generation, not recognizing a season of unique visitation. What a terrible shame! It is no wonder that as many as 75 percent of those converted during that time subsequently fell away.

An older pastor recently told me that about thirty hippies came into his church in the early 1970s, a startling event for his small, conservative Italian Pentecostal church.[23] Thirty hippies would surely stand out. I asked him, "Did you realize that God was doing something special?" He replied, "No. It's just like you said. We didn't know what to do with them. We were a little afraid of them, and they never really got assimilated. After a while, all but one or two left." What an awful loss.

Jesus the Head was moving in dramatic fashion, but the Church, His Body, did not get it. God only knows how different today's world would be if His people had seized the moment. God only knows how many more laborers there would be, how many more godly families, how many more missionaries, how many more Christian leaders, how many more anointed musicians and artists—if only we had awakened to the urgency of the hour and the reality of the Spirit's working. We cannot make this mistake again!/

The prophet Isaiah urged the people of Judah to "seek the LORD while he may be found"; to "call on him while he is near" (Isaiah 55:6), meaning that there are times when He is more readily found than others, and those times must be seized. Hosea exhorted the northern tribes of Israel to turn back to God in repentance, telling them that it was "time to seek the LORD, until he comes and showers righteousness on you" (Hosea 10:12). Soon that time would pass. In the same way Zechariah called on his people to ask the Lord for rain "in the time of the latter rain" (Zechariah 10:1, KJV), "in the season of the spring rain" (NRSV). That season does not last forever.

That is why Jesus wept openly over the city of Jerusalem: "For," He said, "days will come upon you when your enemies will build an embankment around you, surround you and close you in on every side, and level you, and your children within you, to the ground; and they will not leave in you one stone upon another, because you did not know the time of your visitation" (Luke 19:43–44, NKJV). How tragic! The Temple would be destroyed (it remains destroyed more than nineteen hundred years later), the city would be demolished and multitudes would be slain because the people missed the time (Greek, *kairos*) of God's visitation.

With all my heart I believe we are in the early stages of another cultural revolution, a time of great upheaval and shaking, a season of supernatural spiritual seeking, especially among the youth. It does not surprise me,

33

therefore, that the Student Union of Concordia University—one of the largest schools in Canada, with more than 25,000 students on its Montreal campuses—created a stir when it released its 2001/2002 handbook, titled *Uprising*, "with the image of what appears to be a Muslim woman and the word 'revolution' written in several languages on one side."[24] The handbook contains "a page-sized graphic of a plane crashing into an office" (shockingly enough, this handbook was released shortly after Sept. 11, 2001) with the headline: "This is not an agenda called uprising. It is an agenda for uprising." In other words, "Young college radicals, talk is cheap. It's time for action." And what hellish action it could be.

A revolution has already begun, and we cannot afford to sleep through this one. It is time to wake up! As Paul wrote to the believers in Rome almost two thousand years ago: "And do this, understanding the present time. The hour has come for you to wake up from your slumber, because our salvation is nearer now than when we first believed. The night is nearly over; the day is almost here. So let us put aside the deeds of darkness and put on the armor of light" (Romans 13:11–12).

The revolution will not wait.

# 3

# The Church Is Not a Building

---

(AND THE FAMILY IS NOT A HOUSE)

---

Perhaps it is the physical evidence of the Church which most lends credence to the delusion that Christians enjoy a majority status. The alien visitor quickly notices the abundance of ecclesiastical buildings. The average city sky-line is still marked by the presence of spires and, in spite of rising land prices, prominent sites are still occupied by church buildings. . . . Physical appearances may be highly deceptive, especially in something as important as religion. External evidences may go on for a long time after the power of a religion to influence the masses has largely ended.

Elton Trueblood, *The Incendiary Fellowship*

Another thing which is considered of vital importance to the existence of a church is a church building. The thought of a church is so frequently associated with a church building that the building itself is often referred to as "the church." But in God's Word it is the living believers who are called the church, not the bricks and mortar (see Matthew 18:17; Acts 5:11). According to Scripture it is not even necessary for a church to have a place definitely set apart for fellowship.

Watchman Nee, *The Normal Christian Church Life*

The old Ecclesiastical Words to be kept, viz., the Word *Church* not to be translated *Congregation*. . . .

Rule #3 in Richard Bancroft's "Rules to be Observed in the Translation of the [King James] Bible"

The Reformation was a revolt against papal authority but not against the Roman concept of the church as an institution.

William R. Estep, *The Anabaptist Story*

It is the moment you have been waiting for. After months of anticipation, you are about to meet my family. You and I have been friends for months, but you have never set eyes on my family. Today is the big day. I have picked you up at your apartment, and now we are driving together in my car, coming into my neighborhood. In just a few minutes you will get to meet the family.

Of course, your mind is full of questions: What are they like? How will you get along with them? Are they serious? Fun-loving? Friendly? Super-intelligent? Spiritual? Down-to-earth? Soon you will find out.

We turn a corner, drive to the end of the block, park the car and get out. "What do you think?" I ask. "How do you like my family? It's beautiful, isn't it? It took almost two years to build this family, and the inside is more stunning than the outside. It has four big bedrooms and a gorgeous kitchen. Pretty impressive, huh?

You'll love the thick carpets in the family, and those wood floors are really special—not to mention the imported tiles in the foyer. And isn't the brick work fabulous? The workers did a terrific job. Really now, this is quite a family, isn't it?"

What an absurdity! Even to talk like this is silly. It makes no sense at all. A family consists of people, of relationships, of husbands and wives, of moms and dads and brothers and sisters. That is what makes a family.

A family may live in a house, of course, but a family is not a house. And as surely as a family is not a house, *a church is not a building.* Perish the thought. Church means people, community. It is a fellowship of believers, a congregation of the redeemed, a gathering together of the followers of Jesus. This spiritual family may meet in a building, but it is not a building, despite our widespread terminology.

Just think of what our language conveys: "Did you see our new church? It's beautiful!" Or, "It's one of the oldest churches in the city, built in the early 1800s." Or, "Yes, we love our new home, especially since it's only ten minutes from the church."

What does this convey? It says that the church is an edifice you go to one or more times a week, rather than who you and your fellow believers are 24 hours a day, seven days a week. It says that you "attend" the church rather than "are" the church. It equates "building the church" with erecting a physical structure rather than with edifying the Body of Christ.

This makes all the difference in the world since, as William Beckham expressed so concisely, "How we *do* church is directly related to how we *think* church."[1] It also helps to explain why cities can be filled with "churches" (meaning church buildings) without feeling the influence of those "churches" (meaning the people who go to those buildings for Christian services). When we have the "church is a building" mentality, how could it be otherwise? *Going to church* will not change the city; *being the church* will bring about change. This is true in every walk of life. It is how people in secular society bring about change as well.

The reason homosexuals have made such an impact on contemporary culture—influencing the political system, the educational system, the media and the very vocabulary we use—is that they *live* a homosexual lifestyle (and thereby stand for a homosexual agenda). They are not gay one day a week, nor do they merely attend gay meetings. They *are* gay. That is how they make their mark.

On a more wholesome level, consider the civil rights movement. Over a period of many years, civil rights activists held major national rallies, smaller statewide rallies and grassroots community rallies, often in local church buildings. But the rallies were not an end in themselves; they led to action. They did more than raise consciousness and draw people together and call for protests and boycotts. The rallies actually led to protests and boycotts, and those protests and boycotts produced change. Tangible actions produced tangible results.

How successful would the movement have been if it were limited to *going to* civil rights meetings rather than *being* a civil rights movement?

What about the Army? What if the local officers and enlisted members met together once or twice a week and discussed military strategy, displayed the latest weaponry, watched inspirational war films and sang favorite battle songs? And what if attending those meetings became known as "going to the Army"? What kind of Army would we have? How many battles would we win (if we ever made it to battle at all)?

The problem, of course, is the concept of "going to the Army" instead of "being the Army." What a life-and-death difference lies between the two! And what if the Army's meeting place also became known as "the Army"? Confusion would reign, resulting in misguided and misplaced military efforts, since the focus would be on the meeting (not the results of the meeting) and the meeting place (as if a nice building could defeat an enemy). Need I say more? /

Getting back to the Body of Christ, our large, corporate meetings can be wonderfully important, and we should have them as often as we desire or find necessary: They are times of joint worship and praise (which in itself is pleasing to the Lord if done with upright hearts), times of edification and upbuilding (through the corporate "energy" of coming together as a group; through testimonies, preaching and teaching), times of calling for commitment (assuming such messages are preached), times of potential outpouring and visitation.

But they are not an end in themselves, any more than the outpouring on Pentecost in Acts 2 was an end in itself. Rather, the outpouring was given to empower believers to be witnesses, so that Jesus might be glorified and the Great Commission fulfilled, ushering in the Kingdom of God. That divine purpose remains the same. God's agenda has not changed.

Yet the "cathedral" mentality (to use Beckham's expression) works against this, putting the primary emphasis on the large meeting and the large meeting place rather than on the *purpose* of that meeting (with the meeting place simply facilitating the meeting). And with our "church is a building" mindset, we exert incredible amounts of energy and shell out incredible amounts of money and direct incredible amounts of vision toward building an imposing physical structure while we can barely strain out five percent of our budget for foreign missions (five percent would actually be very high for most evangelical churches) or motivate our people to be salt and light in the community. This is not the purpose or meaning of church![2] Yet with all the money spent on some "sanctuaries" these days, I often wonder if some of them are called "worship centers" because they are the places that we worship more than the places in which we worship.

And how often is the typical church building actually used? How much of it, per square foot, is occupied during the week? The most expensive part of the building, the "main sanctuary," is one of the most underused pieces of real estate in the nation. Yet when we have the notion that "the church is a building," we want to build the biggest and most glorious building we can. After all, doesn't Jesus deserve it?

I once saw a cartoon in a Christian magazine that depicted a few birds perched on a telephone wire across the street from a lovely church building, watching as the people left after the Sunday morning service. One bird commented to another, "It's a nice nest. Too bad they only use it once a week." How right those birds were!

Worse still was a special mailing I received from some leaders I did not know (suggesting, perhaps, that they had bought someone else's mailing list, a common practice in "ministry" today), announcing the grand opening of an elaborate new "church" facility compared favorably to the Taj Mahal. This would be a gala affair worth attending from around the nation, an event not to be missed. I imagine the offering that night must have been quite an event, too! Pity the poor believers meeting in storefronts and school gyms, let alone in homes. They will probably never have a Taj of their own.

Yet a further indictment exists: In the first two centuries of this era, the Church experienced great growth without church buildings, and over the last fifty years it has experienced its greatest growth in countries such as Communist China, without church buildings. Most of us would feel crippled without these buildings, despite the fact that God is moving around the world without such structures. Jesus is building His Church without church buildings.

Do I believe buildings have a purpose? Of course. The believers in the book of Acts used them (see, for example, Acts 2:46; 5:12; 19:9–10; the large, corporate gatherings had to assemble somewhere), and they are used today. If we can come together as one, we ought to, not limiting our activities to house meetings. As Watchman Nee noted:

> There was only one church in Jerusalem, but its members assembled in different houses. The principle of houses still applies today. This does not mean that the whole church will always meet separately; in fact, *it is important, and of great profit,* for all the believers to gather together quite regularly in one place (1 Cor. 14:23). To make such meetings possible, they could either borrow or rent a public place for the occasion, or, if they have sufficient means, they could acquire a hall permanently for the purpose.[3]

Yes, large, corporate meetings are important and can be of great profit, and to have such meetings we need to share or rent or own some kind of building. Let's fill them and wear them out until Jesus comes. Buildings are not the problem (unless, of course, they saddle the church with heavy debt). It is the *building mentality* that is so dangerous. As pointed out by New Testament Greek scholars Eugene Nida and J. P. Louw, "In the rendering of *ekklesia* [Greek for "church"] a translator must beware of using a term which refers primarily to a building rather than to a congregation of believers."[4]

41

We desperately need to change our vocabulary, forcing us to change our thinking. We can start by refusing to call the building where we meet a "church." Then we can stop talking about "going to church" or "attending church" or "being late for church." After that we can start referring to the believers with whom we assemble as the "congregation" or "community" of which we are a part. A few little changes can make quite a big difference.

In fact, if you keep speaking about the community of believers you belong to, you will begin to *live* and *function* like a community. The words we use do make a difference.

Go through the entire New Testament and look up every reference to *ekklesia*. Without exception *ekklesia* refers to a people, not a place; to a fellowship, not a facility; to a body, not a building. This, of course, is beyond question, but it takes time and effort to reprogram our thinking. Yet reprogram we must, renewing our minds with the truth of God's Word. This is where the revolution must start—in our very concept of "church."

Greet Priscilla and Aquila, my fellow workers in Christ Jesus. Greet also the church that meets at their house.

Romans 16:3, 5

Give my greetings to the brothers at Laodicea, and to Nympha and the church in her house.

Colossians 4:15

Paul, a prisoner of Christ Jesus, and Timothy our brother, to Philemon our dear friend and fellow worker, to Apphia our sister, to Archippus our fellow soldier and to the church that meets in your home.

Philemon 1–2

Does it jar us to think about "the church" that meets in someone's house? Is this in keeping with our definition of *church*, or do we immediately say to ourselves, "The reason they meet in a home is because they just started that church. When the group gets bigger and more official, it will need to get its own building and put up a sign. Then it will be a church." Is this how we think? If so, we are not thinking biblically. Even if a church has ten thousand "members," when ten of those ten thousand gather in Jesus' name—in a home, in a field, in a school cafeteria—it is a church gathering. Church is taking place!

Jesus required only two or three—not two or three hundred or two or three thousand—to come together in His name for His presence to be there: "Where two or three come together in my name, there am I with them" (Matthew 18:20). Location does not define God's family. A building does not identify the Lord's Church. Rather, two things make the Church the Church: (1) at least two believers gathering in Jesus' name; and (2) the Lord's presence among them. The physical surrounding is immaterial—literally. As Elton Trueblood commented, "It is neither the place nor the setting nor the ritual that is miraculous; it is the fellowship."[5]

Walls do not make a community; ceilings and floors do not make a family; stained-glass windows and padded pews do not make a congregation. God's people make a community, a family, a congregation, a church. And all those churches together make up *the* Church, Messiah's Body.[6] But this is not how most of us think. Instead we follow the model of Constantine who, according to Beckham, brought to a head the cathedral mentality that had been growing over a period of decades:

Using a combination of the Roman governmental and feudal systems, Emperor Constantine developed a church

43

structure that has lasted for seventeen centuries. What are the characteristics of Constantine's paradigm?

People go to a building (cathedral)

on a special day of the week (Sunday)

and someone (a priest, or today, a pastor)

does something to them (teaching, preaching, absolution or healing)

or for them (a ritual or entertainment)

for a price (offerings).[7]

This was not the New Testament believers' mentality. Rather, as Watchman Nee observed:

> The Jews always had their special meeting places, and wherever they went they made a point of building a synagogue in which to worship God. The first apostles were Jews, and the Jewish tendency to build special places of worship was natural to them. Had Christianity [meaning, the new Messianic faith] required that places be set apart for the specific purpose of worshipping the Lord, the early apostles, with their Jewish background and natural tendencies, would have been ready enough to build them. The amazing thing is that, not only did they not put up special buildings, but they seem to have ignored the whole subject intentionally. . . . The temple of the New Testament is not a material edifice; it consists of living persons, all believers in the Lord. Because the New Testament temple is spiritual, the question of meeting places for believers, or places of worship, is one of minor importance.[8]

Sometimes I drive through our cities here in America (especially in the Bible Belt) and ask myself, *What are we doing? What is this thing we call "church"?* We have thousands of church buildings throughout the country, most of which are empty during the week. Then they fill up once or even twice on Sunday, and *possibly* once more in the middle of the week, while people in the surrounding neighborhoods live and die without God. What in the world are we doing?

What makes us think that going to a building, singing a few songs, listening to a nice sermon and giving some money is going to change the world or fulfill the Great Commission or impact the community or threaten the kingdom of darkness? Even if we sing at the top of our lungs, even if we raise our hands and stomp our feet, even if the pastor preaches until his throat gets sore— we still must ask ourselves, *How is this affecting the world?* No wonder the devil pays so little attention to us. If we are happy, he is happy!

Our present state is a very poor representation of the glorious Church for which Jesus died. We hardly demonstrate the power and majesty associated with being His Body, "the fullness of him who fills everything in every way" (Ephesians 1:23). Our corporate potential in Jesus is mighty—we are called to be His fullness on the earth—yet our realization of that potential is meager.

The simple act of moving from a big meeting in a "church" building into a small meeting in a home will not change us in the least. The physical structure in which we meet is not the primary issue. The shift in our mentality is the primary issue. Do we go to church or *are* we the Church? Do we go to a building to watch a religious performance—or, if we are more spiritual, to participate in a religious service—or are we salt and light in our communities, fishers of lost men and women, witnesses for Jesus on a divine mission to glorify God by life or by death?

If we go to a building, let it be to meet with the Lord in depth and power, to be stirred to action and encouraged in our faith, and to strengthen our common bond in Jesus. If we go to a building, let it be to magnify and

45

praise God, then to go into our neighborhoods and workplaces and schools and streets to continue to magnify and praise Him and make Him known there.

Doing this, however, will require a fundamental change in our spiritual orientation, forcing us out of merely attending meetings in "church" buildings once or twice a week and into building relationships as the Church in homes and other smaller settings. It will force us to be the Church wherever we live.

Listen again to Watchman Nee:

> The grand edifices of today, with their lofty spires, speak of the world and the flesh rather than of the Spirit, and in many ways they are not nearly as well suited to the purpose of Christian assembly as the private homes of God's people. In the first place, people feel much freer to speak of spiritual things in the unconventional atmosphere of a home than in a spacious church building where everything is conducted in a formal manner; besides, there is not the same possibility for mutual intercourse there. Somehow, as soon as people enter those special buildings, they involuntarily settle down to passivity, and wait to be preached to. A family atmosphere should pervade all gatherings of the children of God. . . . Further, if the churches are in the private homes of the brethren, they naturally feel that all the interests of the church are their interests. There is a sense of closeness of relationship between themselves and the church. Many Christians feel that church affairs are something quite beyond them. They have no intimate concern in them, because in the first place they have their "minister" who is specially responsible for all such affairs, and then they have a great church building which seems so remote from their homes, and where matters are conducted so systematically and with such precision that one feels overpowered and bound in spirit.
>
> . . . If meetings are in the homes of the Christians, the Church is saved much material loss. One of the reasons

the Christians survived the Roman persecutions during the first three centuries of Church history, was that they had no special buildings for worship, but met in cellars and caves and other inconspicuous places. Such meetings were not readily discovered by their persecutors; but the large and costly edifices of today would be easily located and destroyed, and the churches would be speedily wiped out.[9]

If we want to see God's purposes for His Church fulfilled in our communities, we must come to the place where we realize that we ourselves are God's temple and that God's Spirit lives in us (see 1 Corinthians 3:16); that we are God's building (1 Corinthians 3:9); that in Jesus we are "being built together to become a dwelling in which God lives by his Spirit" (Ephesians 2:22); that we, "like living stones, are being built into a spiritual house to be a holy priesthood, offering spiritual sacrifices acceptable to God through Jesus Christ" (1 Peter 2:5). The Church is a living organism. And this organism, this body, derives its life from Jesus the Head. It is from Him that "the whole body, joined and held together by every supporting ligament, grows and builds itself up in love, as each part does its work" (Ephesians 4:16).

Did you catch those words? Every supporting ligament holds the Church together, and *each part* does its work. Yes, this body is "supported and held together by its ligaments and sinews," and it "grows as God causes it to grow" (Colossians 2:19). To refer once again to a Greek New Testament definition, *ekklesia* is "a congregation of Christians, implying interacting membership"; it is a "gathering of believers" or "group of those who trust in Christ."[10] It is you and I together; it is the family of God; it is the totality of all believers worldwide; it is the local expression of those believers as they gather together in every conceivable location under the sun.

And membership in the Church makes us into "a chosen people, a royal priesthood, a holy nation, a people belonging to God, that [we] may declare the praises of him who called [us] out of darkness into his wonderful light" (1 Peter 2:9).

Freed from the four walls of a building, the Church cannot be limited or contained or destroyed. As Jesus proclaimed, "I will build my church, and the gates of Hades will not overcome it" (Matthew 16:18). Does this sound like something you would like to join?

yes!

11/22/13

# 4

# The Body Is Not an Audience

## (AND THE PREACHER IS NOT A PERFORMER)

In ancient times it was held that men in general could not have direct access to God, that any approach to Him must be mediated by some member of the class of priests, who alone could approach God, and who must accordingly be employed by other men to represent them before Him. This whole conception vanishes in the light of Christianity. By virtue of their relation to Christ all believers have direct approach to God, and consequently, as this right of approach was formerly a priestly privilege, priesthood may now be predicated of every Christian. That none needs another to intervene between his soul and God; that none can thus intervene for another; that every soul may and must stand for itself

49

in personal relation with God—such are the simple elements of the New Testament doctrine of the priesthood
of all believers.

David Estes Foster, "Priesthood in the New Testament"
*International Standard Bible Encyclopedia*

All Christians are truly priests and there is no distinction amongst them except as to office. ... Everybody
who is baptized, may maintain that he has been consecrated as a priest, bishop or pope.

Martin Luther
*To the Christian Nobility*

The image of much of contemporary Christianity could
be summarized as holy people coming regularly to a holy
place on a holy day at a holy hour to participate in a holy
ritual led by a holy man dressed in holy clothes for a
holy fee.

Wolfgang Simson
"Fifteen Theses towards a Re-Incarnation of Church"
*(Houses That Change the World)*

How many times have you heard a pastor begin his message with the words "Turn with me in your Bibles to . . ."?
And how many times have you heard the rustling of
pages as the congregants opened their Bibles to follow
along? Some of us have heard this thousands of times.
In fact, it is common in many churches for almost everyone to bring Bibles—in every size and color—to service
with them.

But call to mind that these scenes would have been
unthinkable six hundred years ago. And remember that
the very thought of believers having access to the Scriptures in their own languages was hotly opposed by
Church leaders for centuries. John Wycliffe was hunted
like a criminal, and William Tyndale was killed for the

crime of translating the Bible into English. And it was "Christian" leaders who persecuted them. Talk about the need for revolution in the Church! How could those professing to be teachers of the Bible end up in such an unbiblical state?

The answer is simple: The Church embraced the false teaching that there are two classes of believers, clergy and laity, and then took that teaching to its logical extreme. Since only the clergy were considered qualified and holy, they alone had access to the Word of God. The effects of that doctrine are still felt today, more than we would like to believe. In this critically important area, we still need a revolution in our churches. Here is some background to give you a clearer picture.

In Old Testament times God set apart a special class of Israelites for divine service. These priests and Levites, the descendants of Aaron and his tribe, had unique access to God. They alone could enter the Holy of Holies, touch the holy things and perform the holy rites, and they alone were anointed for ministry in the Temple of the Lord. All this changed with the death and resurrection of Jesus. He made all believers holy priests, a revolutionary concept in world religions.[1]

Unfortunately this truth was quickly lost; and for centuries, right up to the Reformation, people took for granted that only a special class of Christians was set apart to be priests.[2] This concept undermined the foundations of the new community Jesus was building. And so deeply was this concept ingrained in human nature—the idea that only a select few had direct access to God, while the others were somehow second class, dependent on the elite leaders with their sacred titles and sacred garments—that for a thousand years or more, it seems that no one thought to question it. This led to all kinds of errors in doctrine and practice, and it is why the

51

Church of the Middle Ages hardly resembled the New Testament Church.[3]

The Reformers challenged this doctrine, and a great New Testament truth, commonly known as "the priesthood of all believers," began to be restored.[4] Little by little God's people began to understand that there was *not* a special class of believers who alone enjoyed direct access to God and who alone stood in special closeness to Him. Rather, every child of God had equal access to the Father; every child of God was an equal brother or sister of the Lord Jesus; every child of God was an equal member of the Body; every child of God was a branch of the Vine.

This means that, just as the New Testament does not recognize the concept of special holy buildings, instead calling *all* of us to be the temple of the Lord (both individually and corporately), so also the New Testament does not recognize the concept of special holy people—like Hindu holy men in India—instead calling *all* of us to be holy. In the New Testament Church all believers are priests; all believers are set aside for sacred service; all believers are anointed; all believers have a direct line to heaven; all believers are called saints.[5] All of us!

That is why the gospels, Acts and Hebrews speak of "priests" more than 160 times—as in the Jewish Temple priests, or Jesus the High Priest, or Melchizedek the priest—but never once speak of a special church officer called priest.[6] On the other hand, the few references to priests in 1 Peter and Revelation refer to all believers as part of a holy priesthood, performing priestly functions. All believers!

> As you come to him, the living Stone—rejected by men but chosen by God and precious to him—you also, like living stones, are being built into a spiritual house to be

a holy priesthood, offering spiritual sacrifices acceptable to God through Jesus Christ.

1 Peter 2:4–5

But you are a chosen people, a royal priesthood, a holy
nation, a people belonging to God, that you may declare
the praises of him who called you out of darkness into
his wonderful light.

1 Peter 2:9

As a believer, you are not just a priest in name; you are
a priest in deed, called to offer spiritual sacrifices, called
to intercede, called to declare God's praises. In fact,
Hebrews specifically separates us from the class of
earthly, temple priests, telling us that "we have an altar
from which those who minister at the tabernacle have
no right to eat" (Hebrews 13:10). Our calling is higher!
"Through Jesus, therefore, let us continually offer to
God a sacrifice of praise—the fruit of lips that confess
his name. And do not forget to do good and to share
with others, for with such sacrifices God is pleased"
(Hebrews 13:15–16). Through Jesus you and I have
become "a kingdom and priests to serve his God and
Father" (Revelation 1:6; see also Revelation 5:10; 20:6).[7]
This is spiritual reality.

Yet it is a reality we often fail to grasp, setting up
distinctions the Word does not recognize, using terms
and concepts the Word is against, and putting people
in special outfits and giving them special titles that
only re-erect the wall that the New Testament tore
down. To put it another way, if the minister is a "rev-
erend," what then is the average believer? Is he or she
*just* a believer? To say that is to negate the priesthood
of every believer.

This does not minimize the importance of leaders in the Body. God's Word has much to say about the role of spiritual leaders, laying out the necessary qualifications for leadership and emphasizing their importance in the Church. Without them, the Body will not grow properly; without them, confusion and disorder will result; without them, the Great Commission will not be fulfilled. We need godly leaders. It is Jesus Himself who calls and raises up leaders, and to minimize their role is to minimize the wisdom of the Lord.

The Word also speaks clearly about special callings and ministries—apostles, prophets, evangelists, pastors and teachers, along with elders and deacons. All these are fundamental and essential for healthy church life.

But this does *not* mean there are class distinctions in the Body. It does *not* mean the leaders are "clergy" and the others are "laity." It does *not* mean an elite few are priests and the others are merely commoners. Not at all!

It means the Lord has set within His Body anointed servants to help shepherd the flock. Those who serve well are worthy of respect and honor (1 Thessalonians 5:12–13; 1 Timothy 5:17), their godly example is to be imitated (1 Timothy 4:12; Hebrews 13:7), and they play a key role in equipping their fellow believers for action (Ephesians 4:11–12). Therefore, those who have a bad attitude toward godly authority are simply manifesting their bad attitude toward the authority of God (see Romans 13:2 with regard to secular authority).[8] Leaders carry great responsibility before the Lord.

But they are not mediators between other believers and the Lord, nor do they have an exclusive right to miracles, anointing or divine power, nor are they to be viewed as superstar performers entertaining an enraptured audience. This is not a New Testament picture. But it *is* a picture of much of the contemporary Church.

54

Just look at how our services are structured, as we come together every week primarily to hear one man speak. And look at how we make our leaders the central focus and main attraction, saying things like, "I go to Pastor So-and-so's church." And look at the message conveyed by our church services aired on Christian TV: The leader is the celebrity, the anointed one, the mediator between man and God. The average believer cannot possibly compare with him or her.

Why else would multiplied thousands of believers (who themselves have direct, immediate access to the Father through the blood of Jesus) seem to have more confidence in the special prayers of the man or woman of God on the TV screen (who will lay his or her hands on hundreds of huge stacks of prayer requests) than in the efficacy of their own prayers lifted before the throne of grace?

Which avails more in the sight of God? You as an individual priest taking your petition to the Lord, or a special "holy man" laying his "anointed hands" on a massive pile of prayer requests, including your individual petition?[9] Which prayer is most likely to gain the ear of your Father in heaven? What gets God's attention—personal relationship or powerful anointing? (Remember, the anointing is *His* anointing. It is *His* gift in operation.) God is not impressed by "powerful ministry," since all anointing for ministry is a gift from heaven. Relationship is what He values, and humility impresses Him (see Isaiah 57:15; Micah 6:8).

We have not yet fully embraced the priestly status of every believer. We have not yet rejected the clergy-laity mentality. We need a revolution in our thinking.

It is true that the Scriptures call for the elders to lay hands on the sick (James 5:14–16). But it is equally true that (1) any child of God can come directly to the Father for healing; (2) the Word speaks of elders (plural), not just one leader, indicating that the emphasis is not on a one-man show of any kind; (3) the New Testament also teaches that every believer has the anointing of the Spirit (1 John 2:20), and that the gifts of the Spirit are placed *within the Body* for the common good (1 Corinthians 12:7–11).[10]

Listen to what the noted Greek scholar Edwin Hatch wrote more than one hundred years ago about the nature of the early Church:

> In those early days—before the doors of admission [to the Church] were thrown wide open [to saved and lost alike], before children were ordinarily baptized and men grew up from their earliest years as members of a Christian society, before Christianity had become a fashionable religion and gathered into its net fish "of every kind" both good and bad—the mere membership [in] a Christian Church was in itself a strong presumption of the possession of high spiritual qualifications. The Christian was in a sense which has often since been rather a satire than a metaphor, a "member of Christ," a "king and priest unto God." The whole body of Christians was upon a level: "all ye are brethren" [Matthew 23:8].[11]

This is a profound point. In the beginning, before it was popular to be known as a follower of Yeshua the Messiah, when it was costly to be known as a Christian, when the local assembly of believers actually looked for true evidence of conversion before embracing someone as a brother or sister in the faith, in those days "the mere membership [in] a Christian Church was in itself a strong presumption of the possession of high spiritual qualifications."[12] And it was not a stretch to speak of such people as "members of Christ" and "kings and priests to God." As believers—not as leaders or special church officers—they were blood-bought, redeemed and set apart, and thus "the whole body of Christians was upon [the same] level," all part of the same Body, with Jesus as the only rightful Head.

That's why the Lord so strongly opposed special titles for His disciples, telling them,

> "You are not to be called 'Rabbi,' for you have only one Master and *you are all brothers*. And do not call anyone on earth 'father,' for you have one Father, and he is in heaven. Nor are you to be called 'teacher,' for you have one Teacher, the [Messiah]. The greatest among you will be your servant. For whoever exalts himself will be humbled, and whoever humbles himself will be exalted."
>
> Matthew 23:8–12, emphasis added

You are all brothers: What a radical concept! Teacher and student alike, both brothers; pastor and congregant alike, both brothers; elder and new convert alike, both brothers—equal in status as children of God. Hatch continues:

> The distinctions which St. Paul makes between Christians are based not upon office, but upon varieties of spiritual power. They are caused by the diversity of the operations of the Holy Spirit. They are consequently personal and individual. They do not mark off class from class, but one Christian from another.[13]

How revolutionary some of this *still* sounds: "The distinctions which St. Paul makes between Christians are based not upon office, but upon varieties of spiritual power"—just like a baseball team with nine different players on the field, each playing a different position with different skills, but all of them equally teammates playing together toward a common goal. "They do not mark off class from class, but one Christian from another"—because there is *no class distinction* in the Body.

> Some of these spiritual powers are distinguished from others by a greater visible and outward effect: but they are all the same in kind. The gift of ruling is not different from the gift of healing. The expression 'he that ruleth' is coordinate with 'he that exhorteth,' 'he that giveth,' 'he that sheweth mercy' [Romans 12:6, 8]. Of one or other of these every Christian was a partaker. There was a vivid sense, which in later times was necessarily weakened, that every form of the manifestation of the religious life is a gift of God—a xarisma [*charisma*], or direct operation of the Divine Spirit upon the soul. Now while this sense of the diffusion of spiritual gifts was so vivid, it was impossible that there should be the same sense of distinction between officers [meaning leaders] and non-officers which afterwards came to exist.[14]

Did you grasp the weight of these words? God calls one to lead, one to exhort, one to give, one to show mercy—meaning that *everyone* is called to some area of gifted service in the Body. The one called to a special dimension of giving is just as called as the one called to lead (although the leader has greater responsibility and must therefore meet certain qualifications and live by certain standards).[15] And since the Holy Spirit distributes dynamic gifts in every area of ministry, from administrating to healing, there should not be "the same sense of distinction between officers and non-officers which afterwards came to exist," because everyone is involved in the demonstration of the Spirit's power. Again, I say, these concepts are still revolutionary for most of the Church today.

Yes, a Kingdom is being built, but it is His Kingdom, not the kingdom of a particular minister, just as in any sport, the object for a team is to win, not to realize the goals of one individual player. Players whose primary motivation is to fulfill their personal goals are considered selfish and immature, ultimately working against the common good. It is the same with so many leaders today. Their burning passion is not primarily to build the Messiah's Kingdom, to make His name known and to fulfill His goals as much as it is to fulfill their own vision, rallying people around themselves more than the Lord, guarding their reputations more carefully than they guard the reputation of the Lord. How unscriptural and offensive this is!

Is it good and right for leaders to have clear visions and goals? Absolutely. And they should articulate those visions and goals, planning a strategy and setting it before those they lead. But they must do this as part of the larger picture, part of the Great Commission, part of the extension of God's work on the earth, part of His visions and goals—more than their visions and goals. There can be quite a difference!

But if we fail to see spiritual leaders as respected, senior teammates and fellow workers, helping the rest of the Body to their common Master's work, we will spend the rest of our lives merely supporting "the pastor's vision" rather than finding our place on the team, rolling our sleeves up and getting into the game.

Unfortunately, much of the terminology we use makes the problem even worse. We consider someone in the fellowship who is being used by God to be "just a layman"—meaning, "He's not a professional minister"—as if there was such a biblical concept, as if getting seminary training and being hired by a church and receiving a paycheck makes one a minister of the Gospel, while serving the Lord and bearing fruit for Him without seminary training or a paid church position makes one a layman.

Let's be honest. When we say, "He's just a layman," we really mean, "He's being used by God despite the fact he doesn't know what he's doing. He's actually a businessman or a plumber or a schoolteacher (in other words, more secular than spiritual), yet he's still doing something for the Lord." No wonder the Body is so atrophied. Most of the members are crippled through disuse.

We could also ask if Peter, John and the apostles were "laymen" or "clergy." If they were clergy, at what point did they become clergy? Was it when Jesus called them? Obviously not, since they were called to be disciples, like everyone else. Was it when He designated them as apostles (see Luke 6:12–16)? The text says nothing of the kind, indicating only a call to a special leadership role rather than a change in status. Was it after they were filled with the Spirit on Pentecost? If so, did all the believers in the Upper Room become clergy that day?

By the way, if the baptism in the Spirit makes someone a member of the clergy, then becoming clergy is an act of God, not man, and anyone filled with the Spirit is now a part of the clergy! And if the apostles became clergy at Pentecost (or any time before), why didn't the religious leaders of the day recognize their clerical ordination, stating instead that they were merely "unschooled, ordinary men" (Acts 4:13), or, as rendered in *The Message*, "Their fascination deepened when they realized these two [Peter and John] were laymen with no training in Scripture or formal education"?

No, the New Testament writings do not support our clergy-laity, performer-audience mentality, and Wolfgang Simson did well to observe:

No expression of a New Testament church is ever led by just one professional "holy man" doing the business of communicating with God and then feeding some relatively passive religious consumers Moses-style. Christianity has adopted this method from pagan religions, or at best from the Old Testament.

The heavy professionalization of the church since Constantine has now been a pervasive influence long enough, dividing the people of God artificially into an infantilized laity and a professional clergy, and developing power-based mentalities and pyramid structures. According to the New Testament (1 Tim. 2:5), "there is one God, and one mediator also between God and men, the man Christ Jesus." God simply does not bless religious professionals to force themselves in between Himself and His people.[16]

Yet today, in many charismatic and Pentecostal circles—which often have less of a tendency toward the "professionalization" of the ministry and lack a long history of putting ministers in special robes and giving them special titles—we see an increase in such practices, with new titles coined and new "holy garments" fashioned and the wearing of clerical collars becoming more common.

Now, lest anyone misunderstand me, I need to state clearly that I have no doubt that some of the most godly servants of the Lord today wear priestly robes when they preach or clerical collars through the week, and that some of the most humble men and women of God have special titles before their names. And we must always remember that it is not right for us to make judgments based on outward appearance (see John 7:24) or to judge the motives of someone's heart (see 1 Corinthians 4:1–5; Romans 14:1–13; James 4:11–12).

But it *is* right to ask why people who have no traditional background of this kind would want to move in this direction. On what scriptural basis? To promote what New Testament truth? And it *is* right to ask our liturgical friends—such as Lutherans, Presbyterians and Episcopalians—if their traditional, sacred ministerial garments are in harmony with the message of the Gospel. If the "ministers" should wear priestly robes, shouldn't all believers wear them?[17]

Francis Asbury and Thomas Coke were two of John Wesley's finest workers, ordained by him and sent off to America where they spread the Methodist movement to the point that they were given the title *bishop.* Wesley was utterly appalled:

> I study to be *little;* you study to be *great.* I *creep;* you *strut* along. . . . Do not seek to be *something.* Let me be nothing, and *'Christ be all in all.'*
>
> How can you, how dare you, suffer yourselves to be called BISHOP. I shudder, I start at the very thought! Men may call me a knave or a fool; a rascal, a scoundrel, and I am content. But they shall never, by my consent, call me *Bishop.*[18]

Of course, you can be self-effacing and called *bishop,*[19] or be filled with pride and called by your first name. The question I am asking is this: What is the motivation for wanting to be called by a special title, and do such titles help divide the Body into two classes, clergy and laity?

Even among believers who understand the artificiality of the clergy-laity distinction, widespread misunderstanding prevails, reflected in the common practice of referring to the congregation as "the audience." How often I have heard the phrase, "Now, all you in the audience," and how destructive it is to effective Body life and ministry. The Body is not an audience! The words do not even make sense when used together in the same sentence. Yet this is how we *think.*

And what does an audience do? Nothing more than enjoy the show, unless it is a lively audience, in which case it sometimes participates—as much as spectators can participate. But audience participation is not the same as active obedience. Instead, it is like the hands clapping when the mouth receives a signal from the brain and says to the whole body, "Get up and run." Clapping is not running, and saying *Amen!* when the Word is preached is not obeying. That is why James warned his readers of the dangers of being hearers of the Word rather than doers of the Word, thereby "deceiving themselves" (James 1:22, NKJV). By going to a service and singing along with the choir and saying *Amen!* to the preacher, we give ourselves the impression that we are actually doing something, when we are merely being an audience, thereby deceiving ourselves. Jesus did not save us and call us to be an audience!

Audiences do not change the world. Audiences do not start revolutions. Audiences do not advance the Kingdom. Audiences do not fulfill the Great Commission. And audiences do not threaten the devil one bit. We must destroy this audience mentality, although our entertainment-oriented culture, replete with slick megachurches and superstar-preachers, makes this an uphill battle for sure. But change we must, since the devil's troops understand well how the battle must be won—and it is *not* with the audience mentality.

House church advocate Frank Viola points out that

> . . . every time Paul wrote to a church (the Pastorals to one side, for they are personal letters written to Paul's *apostolic* co-workers), he always addresses *the church itself* rather than its leaders (Rom. 1:7; 1 Cor. 1:1–2; 2 Cor. 1:1; Gal. 1:1–2; Eph. 1:1; Phil. 1:1; Col. 1:1–2; 1 Thess. 1:1; 2 Thess. 1:1). This trend is highlighted in the book of Hebrews, where the writer off-handedly tells the saints to greet their leaders for him at the close of his letter (Heb. 13:24).

More striking, if we examine the most troubled church mentioned in the NT, the Corinthian assembly, Paul never once appeals to its leadership. Throughout the entire Corinthian correspondence, Paul never chastises the elders, nor commends obedience to them. In fact, he doesn't even mention them! Instead, Paul appeals solely to the saints and reminds them of *their responsibility* to the saints and reminds them of *their responsibility* to deal with the church's own self-inflicted wounds.[20]

You might read this and think to yourself, *Paul was writing as a leader to these churches; that's why he didn't address the leaders.* But that begs the question since: (1) Paul was not the primary leader or final authority figure in every one of these churches; (2) even if he was "the apostle" over all these churches (which is not an accurate concept), according to the clergy-laity mentality, he still should have addressed the local leaders and told *them* to tell their people what to do; and (3) even if he was writing as the final authority over all these churches (which he was not), the bottom line is that he told all the members of the local body what to believe, how to live and what to do—because the body is not an audience.

As Viola points out:

The stress of the NT, then, is upon *corporate* responsibility. It is the *believing community* that is called to organize itself (1 Cor. 11:33–34; 14:39–40; 16:2–3); discipline fallen members (1 Cor. 5:3–5; 6:1–6); warn the unruly (1 Thess. 5:14); comfort the feeble (1 Thess. 5:14); support the weak (1 Thess. 5:21); abound in the work of the Lord (1 Cor. 15:58); admonish one another (Rom. 15:14); teach one another (Col. 3:16); prophesy to one another (1 Cor. 14:31); serve one another (Gal. 5:13); bear one another's burdens (Gal. 6:2); care for one another (1 Cor. 12:25); wash one another's feet (John

64

13:14); love one another (John 13:34–35; 15:12, 17; Rom. 13:8; 1 Thess. 4:9); be devoted to one another (Rom. 12:10); show kindness and compassion to one another (Eph. 4:32); edify one another (Rom. 14:19; 1 Thess. 5:11b); bear with one another (Eph. 4:2; Col. 3:13); exhort one another (Heb. 3:13; 10:25); incite one another to love and good works (Heb. 10:24); encourage one another (1 Thess. 5:11a); pray for one another (Jas. 5:16); offer hospitality to one another (1 Pet. 4:9); fellowship with one another (1 John 1:7); and confess sins to one another (Jas. 5:16).[21]

As full as this listing is, it barely includes any of the other aspects of Body ministry that Paul writes about elsewhere, such as being used in spiritual gifts like healing and miracles (see 1 Corinthians 12–14) or being used in giving or exhorting or showing mercy or leading, which is just another aspect of service and gifting for members of the Body (Romans 12:3–8).[22]

To repeat: There *is* a critically important place for leaders in the Church, as Paul exhorted the Thessalonians: "Dear brothers and sisters, honor those who are your leaders in the Lord's work. They work hard among you and warn you against all that is wrong. Think highly of them and give them your wholehearted love because of their work" (1 Thessalonians 5:12–13, NLT). Or, as Hebrews says, "Remember your leaders, who spoke the word of God to you. Consider the outcome of their way of life and imitate their faith" (Hebrews 13:7).

But leaders do not belong to a different spiritual class than the rest of the congregation, nor are they of a different spiritual substance than the rest of the Body. Not at all! Leaders are members of the Body who also take orders from Jesus the Head. He is the ultimate one in charge! And the function of church leaders is like the function of the coach of a sports team. The coach is expected to be more mature and experienced than the players; the coach knows the game well through lots of practical experience and hard work; the coach helps train and motivate and equip the team. But the team plays the game; the team wins or loses; the team makes things happen; the team is what people come to see.[23]

Just think how our nation could be shaken if the tens of millions of believers in the land today got off the sidelines and onto the front lines, out of the audience and into the action, rising up as holy priests called and anointed by God, ministering to the needs of a lost generation.

But being a priest means bearing responsibility. Being a priest means separating from sin. Being a priest means intimacy with God. So what it will be? Will you be a pew-sitter or will you be a priest?

11/23/13

# 5

# Cult-Like or Cutting-Edge?

WHAT IT REALLY MEANS TO BE A DISCIPLE

Large crowds were traveling with Jesus, and turning to them he said: "If anyone comes to me and does not hate his father and mother, his wife and children, his brothers and sisters—yes, even his own life—he cannot be my disciple. And anyone who does not carry his cross and follow me cannot be my disciple."

Luke 14:25–27

Simply put, if you're not willing to take what is dearest to you, whether plans or people, and kiss it goodbye, you can't be my disciple.

Luke 14:33, MESSAGE

... the number of disciples was increasing. ... The number of disciples in Jerusalem increased rapidly. ... They preached the good news in that city and won a large number of disciples. ... The disciples were called Christians first at Antioch.

Acts 6:1, 7; 14:21; 11:26

If indeed we lived a life in imitation of his, our witness would be irresistible. If we dared to live beyond our self-concern, if we refused to shrink from being vulnerable, if we took nothing but a compassionate attitude toward the world, if we were a counterculture to our nation's lunatic lust for pride of place, power, and possessions, if we preferred to be faithful rather than successful, the walls of indifference to Jesus Christ would crumble. A handful of us could be ignored by society, but hundreds, thousands, millions of such servants would overwhelm the world. Christians filled with the authenticity, commitment, and generosity of Jesus would be the most spectacular sign in the history of the human race. The call of Jesus is revolutionary. If we implemented it, we would change the world in a few months.

Brennan Manning, The Signature of Jesus

Commitment is not fanaticism. In substance, the twelfth chapter of Romans says: "I urge you to present your life to Jesus Christ as a living sacrifice, acceptable to God— which is a reasonable, normal action on your part." That's not fanatical. In fact, you're not "normal" or reasonable until you've made that kind of commitment.

Tom Skinner, Words of Revolution

One of the things that holds many of us back is the fear of going too far, of crossing over the line, of going off the deep end, of becoming cult-like and fanatical, of losing touch with reality. The memories of Jonestown and Heaven's Gate are all too real to us, and we have heard more than enough stories of demonized parents or children who murdered their own flesh and blood because "God told them to." We have seen our share of Hare Krishna devotees chanting on street corners, or sleep-deprived young people selling flowers eighteen hours a day, or sweet-talking cult members knocking on our doors, eager to share their faith but incapable of thinking for themselves. We don't want to become like that!

And for good reason. God does not brainwash His children. He does not lobotomize us when we get saved and remove our capacity to think. He does not immobilize our minds and reduce us to robotic obedience. He does not call us to abusive and destructive acts, such as beating our bodies or mutilating ourselves in some bizarre attempt to subdue the flesh. And He certainly does not call us to submit every part of our lives—down to our innermost, secret thoughts—to the whims and demands of an earthly leader. All these things are characteristic of cults, bringing people into bondage and captivity. That is not the Jesus way. Jesus sets the captives free.

But there is another side to the story. Jesus demands radical, absolute obedience from His followers, an obedience so extreme that to most of the world (and much of the Church) it appears fanatical, even cult-like. Jesus calls us to be His disciples. Do we really know what this means?

For most of us, the answer is no. We have taken the punch out of the word so that the thought of being a disciple does not seem too threatening. After all, don't most serious believers want to be "discipled"? Isn't one of the great needs in the Body today the need for more discipling? A disciple is a devoted learner and a devoted follower. Who doesn't want to be a disciple?

Perhaps we are asking the wrong questions. Perhaps it would be better to ask, "Who wants to be a disciple of

*Jesus?"* That puts everything in a different light. Are you sure you want to be one of *His* disciples?

Many of us are at home with the concept of being Christians. Yet the word *Christian* occurs only three times in the entire New Testament, once in Acts 11 (at Antioch, where the disciples were first called Christians); once in Acts 26 (where Agrippa asks Paul if he thinks he can persuade him to be a Christian in such a short time); and once in 1 Peter 4 (where Peter tells the believers not to be ashamed of suffering reproach because they are called Christians). In New Testament times, not only was the term *Christian* rare, but it was used (most scholars agree) in a derogatory sense. Being called a Christian was anything but a compliment. It meant being one of *them*. Wearing that name meant bearing reproach.

How different things are today! The great majority of Americans consider themselves Christians. The name is common, the name has been cheapened and the name is hardly negative. To identify yourself as a Christian carries very little meaning and costs almost nothing, unless you came to Jesus from Islam or Hinduism or some other religion and you are telling someone from your old religion about your new faith.

The Word of God never calls people to "become Christians," especially as we commonly use the term. And the goal of the Great Commission is not to win people to a new religion, which is what "becoming a Christian" means to most people today. Rather, it is a call to make disciples—true disciples, obedient to the Lord. As Jesus commanded, "Go and make disciples of all nations, baptizing them in the name of the Father and of the Son and of the Holy Spirit, and teaching them to obey everything I have commanded you. And surely I am with you always, to the very end of the age" (Matthew 28:19–20).

Has this Commission ever changed? Has anyone overruled the Lord and come up with a new and better plan?

By what authority have we left off making disciples and taken up getting "decisions," or signing up people for church membership, or getting people "saved" and stopping there? Who changed what Jesus commanded? What else have we to do on earth but become disciples and make disciples?

"Being a Christian" is not a New Testament emphasis, nor does it communicate today what it did in the days of the apostles. Even the concept of being a "believer"—a word used thirteen times in Acts and thirteen times in the rest of the New Testament—is hardly challenging for us. What does it actually cost to be a believer? What sacrifice is entailed? In America today, almost everyone believes in Jesus.

The issue for us is not so much being a "Christian" or a "believer" but rather being a "disciple"—a term used more than 260 times in the entire New Testament (including more than 230 times in the gospels and 28 times in Acts). How can we downplay or ignore the call to true discipleship when it is such a prominent theme in the Word?

What does it tell us when the word *Christian* occurs just three times in the New Testament and the term *believer* only 26 times, but there are more than 260 references to *disciples,* with clear explanations about what this means? What does it tell us when most of us would have no problem saying, "I'm a Christian," or, "I'm a believer," but would have a much harder time saying, "I'm a disciple"? Just saying the words out loud causes us to examine ourselves afresh. "Am I *really* a disciple?"

Remember the culture of the New Testament world. *Rabbi* was not a formal title or clerical office at the time. It was a term of honor applied to special teachers and leaders. These rabbis had followers, devoted students who would flock around their teacher/leader/master. Rabbi Yohanan the Immerser (John the Baptist) had his

71

followers; Rabbi Yeshua (Jesus) had His. Scripture even records that "the Pharisees heard that Jesus was gaining and baptizing more disciples than John" (John 4:1; see also John 3:25).

A disciple was identified with his master. His whole world revolved around his leader. "A student [disciple] is not above his teacher, but everyone who is fully trained will be like his teacher" (Luke 6:40). "A student [disciple] is not above his teacher, nor a servant above his master. It is enough for the student [disciple] to be like his teacher, and the servant like his master" (Matthew 10:24–25). Yes, to be like one's teacher—that would be enough!

Have you ever seen pictures of an Indian guru with a band of loyal disciples? They follow him everywhere. They sit at his feet and devour his every word. They watch his every move and try to emulate his attitude and conduct. They carry his picture with them, gaze at him lovingly and esteem him beyond all proportion and reality. "Master! Swami!"[1] They want to be like him. If they could only be half the man their leader is, if they could only be faithful miniatures of their master, they would be thrilled beyond words. Their lives are absorbed in his, and their whole identity comes from him. That is the picture of a disciple.

In the early 1980s I worked as a salesman for a small company. One of my colleagues was a man I will call Sam. We were a study in contrasts. I was a devoted follower of Jesus; he was a devoted follower of an "enlightened" American teacher named (at that time) Da Free John. Sam was certainly devoted. Part of his religious discipline included a strict vegetarian diet, so even when we had a business luncheon with potential customers, he would open his briefcase and take out some carefully packed food that looked more like leftover dog food and seaweed. Can you imagine someone doing that at a restaurant while courting new customers? But Sam did it without shame. In fact, I believe he did it with pride. He was a disciple! He was glad to be different. He was glad to stand out. It identified him with his master.

Sam's daily routine included another interesting practice: He would prostrate himself on the ground and meditate. Our boss, Stu, learned about this while taking a business trip with Sam. Stu spotted him lying on his face on the grass in front of a post office. It was the first free moment in the day that Sam could find. Not surprisingly, this drew the attention of the postmaster, who pointed out to Stu with some amusement, "That's where all the dogs go!" But Sam was not deterred. He lived to carry out his master's orders. (As a sidelight to this story I should mention that all three of us—Stu, Sam and I— were Jews.)

One day we learned that Sam and his wife planned to move to a small island thousands of miles away. Their master decided he wanted them there to carry out his work. As far as I know, they went without hesitation. Anything else would have been the height of disloyalty, unworthy of a true disciple.

"But that's cult-like!" you say. "That's not the Jesus way."

Yes and no. The absurdity of the practices, the false enlightenment of the leader and the deceptive powers at work were all cult-like, for sure. But Sam's unquestioning devotion toward his master was perfectly normal for a true disciple. Jesus demanded this and more. Come and see what the Scriptures teach.

The original twelve disciples of Jesus stayed constantly by the Lord's side. Where He was, they were. At times it is almost comical, as if they were virtually tripping over Him, and the only way He could get alone was to get up very early (Mark 1:35) or stay up really late (Luke 6:12). They were closer to Him than His own family (Matthew 12:48–50), and He shared His secrets with them, even sending them out to represent Him (Matthew 10:40) and carry out His mission (Matthew 10:7–8).[2]

But the gospels do not speak only of the Twelve. In fact, the majority of references to "disciples" are not to the Twelve but to the many other men and women who followed Him. Jesus did not make it easy for them!

> When Jesus saw the crowd around him, he gave orders to cross to the other side of the lake. Then a teacher of the law came to him and said, "Teacher, I will follow you wherever you go." Jesus replied, "Foxes have holes and birds of the air have nests, but the Son of Man has no place to lay his head." Another disciple said to him, "Lord, first let me go and bury my father." But Jesus told him, "Follow me, and let the dead bury their own dead."
>
> Matthew 8:18–22

Whatever these verses mean, this much is sure: In order to be one of Rabbi Yeshua's disciples, personal convenience had to be crucified, personal bonds had to be broken and personal loyalties had to be left behind. No honest interpretation can cheapen the radical nature of the calling. The Lord simply made things too clear:

> "Anyone who loves his father or mother more than me is not worthy of me; anyone who loves his son or daughter more than me is not worthy of me; and anyone who does not take his cross and follow me is not worthy of me. Whoever finds his life will lose it, and whoever loses his life for my sake will find it."
>
> Matthew 10:37–39

Did you notice those words *not worthy of Me?* The eternal Word-made-flesh cuts no deals. Being one of His disciples is the highest calling known to man, and through His death for us (that's right, the sinless Master dies for the sinful disciples), we become part of His family, adopted by His Father and made joint-heirs with our Lord. He has every right to set the standards high. No other master is like our Master, no lord like our Lord. Who gave us the right to modify what He said?

After Jesus told His disciples He would suffer and die and rise from the dead in Jerusalem, and after He rebuked Peter for rebuking *Him*, the Lord made a universal declaration:

> "If anyone would come after me, he must deny himself and take up his cross and follow me. For whoever wants to save his life will lose it, but whoever loses his life for me will find it. What good will it be for a man if he gains the whole world, yet forfeits his soul? Or what can a man give in exchange for his soul? For the Son of Man is going to come in his Father's glory with his angels, and then he will reward each person according to what he has done."
>
> Matthew 16:24–27

Jesus said, "If anyone would come after me"—*anyone* meaning young or old, male or female, black or white, rich or poor, educated or illiterate—he or she must do three things: (1) deny himself, saying no to self-will, personal desires and fleshly lusts; (2) take up his cross, dying to the old life and all its claims, with implications of rejection, shame and suffering; and (3) follow Me.[3] As expressed clearly by the *New International Dictionary of New Testament Theology*, "Following Jesus as a disciple means the unconditional sacrifice of his whole life . . . for the whole of his life. . . . To be a disciple means (as Matthew in particular emphasizes) to be bound to Jesus and to do God's will (Matthew 12:46–50; cf. Mark 3:31–35)."[4]

What a statement!—*the unconditional sacrifice of his whole life for the whole of his life*. That's it! That is what it means to be a disciple. Everything for Jesus, always and forever. No excuses, no exemptions, no exceptions.

"I will follow you, Lord," a man said to Jesus as He walked by, "but first let me go back and say good-by to my family." Jesus replied, "No one who puts his hand to the plow and looks back is fit for service in the kingdom of God" (Luke 9:61–62).

This was the expected pattern:

> Jesus went out and saw a tax collector by the name of Levi sitting at his tax booth. "Follow me," Jesus said to him, and Levi got up, left everything and followed him.
>
> Luke 5:27–28

> As Jesus was walking beside the Sea of Galilee, he saw two brothers, Simon called Peter and his brother Andrew. They were casting a net into the lake, for they were fishermen. "Come, follow me," Jesus said, "and I will make you fishers of men." At once they left their nets and followed him. Going on from there, he saw two other brothers, James son of Zebedee and his brother John. They were in a boat with their father Zebedee, preparing their nets. Jesus called them, and immediately they left the boat and their father and followed him.
>
> Matthew 4:18–22

He called, and they left everything and followed Him.[5] That, in a nutshell, is a picture of discipleship, of true devotion. That is the New Testament norm. And "the call to be a disciple always includes the call to service."[6] As expressed by Messianic Jewish scholar Dan Gruber, from a biblical standpoint, rather than asking someone, "Are you saved?" we should ask, "Who are you serving?" There is quite a difference.

Jesus taught plainly that "any of you who does not give up everything he has cannot be my disciple" (Luke 14:33), a verse called by the late evangelist and activist Tom Skinner "one of the toughest verses in the Scriptures," noting that "many people wish it wasn't there." Skinner continued: "There are those people who say, 'Well, God doesn't mean for us to give up everything. I can follow Christ and do my thing without giving up everything.' They say, 'What the Bible really means is that we should be *willing* to.' Check out that verse—do you see the word *willing*?"[7]

For many of us there is a great mental disconnect when we read certain portions of the Bible. The gospels are one thing; the rest of the New Testament is quite another. The Jesus of the gospels is so "out there" in His demands. His teachings always seem to need some kind of explanation or modification. Isn't this how we think, either consciously or unconsciously?

"This kind of stuff was okay for His first followers," we may say. "They could literally leave everything and go with Him, even to death. For us it's different. After all, *they* were the disciples. *We* are just believers, members of a local church." Our faith is more comfy than costly, more dainty than dangerous, more reasonable than radical, more life-enhancing than life-threatening. Things are different now. Things have changed. Right?

Not in terms of God's will and God's ways. Not in terms of God's demands and God's desires. Not in terms of God's requirements and God's regulations. A disciple is a disciple, and it was this term—more than *believer* and far more than *Christian, saved, witness* or *saint*—that most often designated the members of the Body in the book of Acts. The believers were the disciples; the saved were the disciples; the Christians were the disciples. (Remember the words of Acts 11:26: "The *disciples* were called *Christians* first at Antioch.") If you were a

77

believer you were a disciple—and Jesus made plain what it meant to be a disciple.

Now I ask you, in all honesty: What book, what institution, what leader has the right to tell us that Jesus did not mean what He said, that His explicit demands applied only to a select few, that His first followers were somehow cut from different cloth than His twenty-first-century followers? On what basis do we dilute the Master's words?

We read what He required in the gospels, and we see how the disciples responded in Acts, giving up everything for His cause and going against the grain of the religious establishment, even at the cost of their lives. The epistles confirm all this, challenging us to offer our lives as a well-pleasing sacrifice to the Lord (for example, Romans 12:1–2; Ephesians 5:1–2; 1 Corinthians 6:20). At what point did Jesus, completely apart from the written Word, lower the standard? At what point did He redefine what it means to be worthy of following Him? At what point did He change the requirements for being a disciple?

You may ask, "Are you saying, then, that we need to quit our jobs, drop out of school, leave our families, sell our possessions, put a few cans of food into a backpack and go hiking into the wilderness somewhere 'with Jesus'?"

Hardly. But I am saying you must reorient your whole life so that living for the Lord becomes your all-consuming passion, the preeminent force in your life, that which drives you and motivates you, the standard by which every other area of life is judged and the criterion by which everything is evaluated. That is what it means to be a disciple. It means being utterly absorbed with Jesus and His mission. It means a total revolution in your life and the total consecration of your life to the Jesus revolution.[8]

What if you were a secular revolutionary devoted to overthrowing the wealthy elite? What if this was your cause, your life? What if you had a job as a factory worker, laboring twelve hours a day? What would motivate you? Would getting ahead on your job be your central focus? Would owning a lovely home in the suburbs be your primary goal? Certainly not! Instead, your primary goal would be fomenting the revolution. You would seek to educate your co-workers, give them revolutionary tracts and tapes, share revolutionary concepts with them, incite within them the revolutionary spirit, invite them to revolutionary meetings.

"We've got to change the system," you would say. "We've got to increase our numbers and organize our efforts and sharpen our strategy. And when the time is right, we'll make our move!"

If you had extra money, you would invest it in the revolution. If you decided to get married, you would marry a fellow revolutionary. If you had children, you would rear them to be revolutionaries. Like all true revolutionaries, you would rather sacrifice and even die for the cause than accept the status quo. As expressed by Elaine Brown, speaking of her days as leader of the militant Black Panthers: "It was invigorating. It made life important. It made it bigger than you. Even the notion of dying for something bigger than you was far more powerful than living out a life of quiet desperation. I was the happiest in my life when I was in the Black Panther Party."[9]

What then should our attitude be as members of the Jesus People Party? How then should we live? The Kingdom of God has broken into this world, and the King Himself has enlisted us in His cause, entrusting the keys of that Kingdom to us and calling us to overthrow the powers of darkness and liberate captives in His name. What kind of lifestyle makes sense?[10]

Dr. Bill Bright observed that

Nechayev, a Marxist of the last century, who died in prison for his role in the assassination of Czar Alexander II, said, "The revolutionary man is a consecrated man. He has neither his own interest nor concerns nor feelings, no attachments nor property, not even a name. All for him is absorbed in the single exclusive interest, in the one thought, in the one passion—revolution."

But this quality of dedication was not original with the Marxists or communists of today. It was Jesus who said: "If any one desires to be My disciple, let him deny himself—that is, disregard, lose sight of and forget himself and his own interests—and take up his cross and follow Me (. . . conform wholly to My example in living and if need be in dying also)."

This means that the one who wishes to follow Him as His disciple must be willing to forfeit all claim to his life and make Christ and His kingdom paramount to all his consideration. That the Apostle Paul had done this, along with multiplied thousands of other Christians, is apparent as he refers to himself in the first chapter of the book of Romans as a "bondslave of Jesus."[11]

A disciple, by definition, is a bondslave of the Lord, totally dedicated to the Master, having left all for the (revolutionary) cause.[12]

The first believers were identified with "the Way." It spoke of something different and exclusive. It branded them as part of a narrow and definite cause. The world had its many ways; religion had its many ways; the believers had *the Way*.[13]

Before meeting the Lord, Saul of Tarsus sought to persecute all "who belonged to the Way, whether men or women, [that] he might take them as prisoners to Jerusalem" (Acts 9:2). Later in life he called himself "a follower of the Way" (Acts 24:14). Felix, who supervised

Paul's trial, was "well acquainted with the Way" (Acts 24:22). In the city of Ephesus, people "publicly maligned the Way" and "there arose a great disturbance about the Way" (Acts 19:9, 23).

This Way went against the grain. This Way was countercultural in the fullest sense of the word. This Way was costly and dangerous. But this was the only Way! How should we live as followers of the Way?[14] It really does separate us from the rest of the world, and it really does separate us to the Lord. Devotion to Him is the beginning and middle and end of discipleship.

Think back to the early days. Was there ever a time in your life that you had a "first love" relationship with the Lord? Jesus was so real to you, so precious to you, so fulfilling to you, that nothing else mattered. He was your life! His opinion was the only opinion that mattered. His favor meant more than all the favor of the world. Everything around you could be dark and gloomy, but His smile would brighten your day. And telling others about Him came naturally, out of the overflow of your heart. You had to try *not* to talk about Him so much rather than force yourself to share the Good News.

That is what it means to be absorbed with the Lord, to be sold out to Jesus, to leave everything for Him, to be a disciple. The Master's call is absolute.

Notice in Matthew 28 that it was "the eleven disciples" who met with Jesus and heard His Great Commission. They were the ones who heard Him say, "All authority in heaven and on earth has been given to me. Therefore go and make disciples of all nations, baptizing them in the name of the Father and of the Son and of the Holy Spirit." They were the ones who heard Him say that they were to teach the new disciples to "obey everything I have commanded you" (Matthew 28:17–20). In other words, they were to *reproduce themselves,* disciples of Jesus reproducing disciples of Jesus.

81

As faithful disciples they obeyed: "After the Lord Jesus had spoken to them, he was taken up into heaven and he sat at the right hand of God. Then *the disciples* went out and preached everywhere, and the Lord worked with them and confirmed his word by the signs that accompanied it" (Mark 16:19–20, emphasis added).

They had seen the Lord Jesus while He walked on earth. They had seen God incarnate in action. His power was so incredible, His majesty so indescribable, His wisdom so irrefutable, His compassion so unfathomable, that they joyfully left everything to follow Him. What a privilege it was to be one of His disciples! At times the crowds were so overwhelming He had to get into a boat and move away from the shoreline to avoid being crushed by the multitudes who gathered to "hear him and to be healed of their sicknesses" (Luke 5:15; see also Matthew 13:1–2). One time some people bringing a paralyzed man actually took the roof off a house to reach Jesus, being unable to press through the crowds (see Mark 2:1–12).

When people learned that Jesus had arrived in their region,

> they ran throughout that whole region and carried the sick on mats to wherever they heard he was. And wherever he went—into villages, towns or countryside—they placed the sick in the marketplaces. They begged him to let them touch even the edge of his cloak, and all who touched him were healed.
>
> Mark 6:55–56

What a Savior! But none of the disciples understood what was happening when He was betrayed, arrested, rejected, mocked and crucified. They did not expect their Messiah to die a criminal's death. How could this be? They did not understand He was dying *for them.*

82

Who could conceive such a thing? And then, in their most hopeless hour, when it seemed their dreams had been nothing but empty clouds, their Master rose from the dead! He overcame the grave! He broke Satan's back! He triumphed!

Afterward Jesus mingled with them and taught them for forty days, finally ascending to heaven in a cloud right before their eyes. Then He sent His Spirit upon them, enabling them to do the very same things He had done. This was too good to be true—but it *was* true!

*Of course* they went and preached everywhere. *Of course* they told everyone the Good News. *Of course* they were willing to give their lives for the cause. After all, they were disciples. Are you?

# 6

# Revolutionary, Not "Rebelutionary"

## FOLLOWING THE JESUS PATTERN

Was Jesus a revolutionist? That was our question. We can answer it only with a *sic et non*, with yes *and* no. He cannot be party to those who—then as now—seek to improve the world by violence, a violence which begins with a hate-filled defamation and escalates to bloody terror, to torture and mass murder, where one party shifts all the blame on the opponent. The Jewish War (A.D. 66–70) is a striking paradigm for that. The errors of church history, crusades, inquisition, and religious wars, should put us on guard, today especially, against a romantic justification of revolutionary violence. . . . Jesus pointed a quite different way with *agape:* the way of nonviolent protest and willingness to suffer, a way

84

which deserves more fully the designation 'revolution-ary' than does the old, primitive way of violence. Dur-ing his activity of one or two years he was a greater rev-olutionary force in world and intellectual history than all agents of revolutionary violence from Spartacus and Judas the Galilean till today.

Martin Hengel, *Was Jesus a Revolutionist?*

The voice crying in the wilderness demanded a way for the Lord, a way prepared, and a way prepared in the wilderness. I would be attentive to the Master's procla-mation, and give him a road into my heart, cast up by gracious operations, through the desert of my nature. . . . Stumbling-blocks of sin must be removed, and thorns and briers of rebellion must be uprooted. So great a visi-tor must not find miry ways and stony places when he comes to honour his favoured ones with his company.

Charles H. Spurgeon,
*Morning and Evening: Daily Readings*
January 3, commenting on Luke 3:4

If we are really going to see a spiritual revolution, we must be a spiritual army, and if we are really going to be a spiritual army, we must be a people submitted to authority. Otherwise there will be a revolution, but not a Jesus revolution. It will be a revolution of the flesh, a revolution of rebellion, pride, self-will, independence, retaliation and anger—everything other than the Spirit of God. It will not be born in heaven but will be "earthly, unspiritual, of the devil" (James 3:15).

That is *not* the revolution we need, and I for one want no part of it. It bears no resemblance to the character and substance of a God-sent, Spirit-led, Jesus-initiated, world-changing, holy movement.

One revolution has the smell of the world; the other has the aroma of heaven. In the social realm, one revolution fights fleshly evils with fleshly efforts; the other overcomes evil with good. In the spiritual realm, one revolution responds to dead tradition with pride and elitism; the other brings life and transformation. One rejects old wineskins in favor of reactionary substitutes; the other is modeled by God, building His house His way. We must get this right!

In the next three chapters we will deal with one of the greatest hindrances to Church revolution in our day— namely, *the abuse of spiritual authority.* This power-mongering, controlling mentality stands against liberty in the Spirit, against forward progress in the things of God, against the prophetic word from heaven, against dynamic spiritual growth and vitality. It must be confronted and dismantled.

But before we can tackle that stronghold, we must address an equally formidable foe: the lack of submission to godly authority; the spirit of lawlessness and disorder, with everyone doing what is right in his or her own eyes.[1] When our goal is spiritual revolution, we must be especially careful, since being revolutionary means going against the grain, resisting the establishment, rejecting the status quo, bringing an unpopular prophetic message, forging a new path as pioneers— and every one of these is a potential trap for the sinful nature. Every one of these can easily be mixed with rebellion and mingled with the flesh.

Fellow revolutionaries, beware! The Jesus way is not easy. The Jesus way means crucifixion before resurrection and humiliation before exaltation. The Jesus way means radical submission to God, turning the other cheek to offenses, suffering misunderstanding and rejection, being mocked and ridiculed and scorned—without fighting back in the flesh. It means waiting patiently for God's vindication, seeking His face until the answer comes, overcoming the strength and wisdom of "the system" with the weakness and foolishness of the cross.

But it is the only real way to change the world, the only real way to impact a generation for good, the only real way to advance the Kingdom of God. To say it again: We must get this right!

Young people in particular need to hear this clearly, since within youth—especially through the teen years and into the twenties—there is an innate tendency to resist authority, to push against boundaries, to challenge restrictions, to question standards, to test limitations, to desire change for the sake of change alone, to experiment and search and try new things, to rebel. That is why college campuses have been hotbeds for worldly revolutions, and why a slogan from the 1960s counterculture movement was, "Don't trust anybody over thirty."[2] But that is not the slogan of the Jesus movement of today.

Today's Jesus movement is built on Malachi 4:6, God turning the hearts of the fathers to the children and the children to the fathers. It is built on the joining of generations. It is built on true fathers nurturing godly offspring and solid disciples. It is built on understanding and compassion from the parents (both spiritual and natural) and on respect and obedience from the daughters and sons. It is built on family, community, mutual subjection, gentleness of spirit and meekness of heart. It is built on Jesus Himself—and that means the way of submission.

Despite being the Son of God, Jesus obeyed His earthly parents (Luke 2:51). Despite being the Judge of the living and the dead, He submitted Himself to the judgment of corrupt earthly rulers, even to the point of death on the cross (Philippians 2:5–11). Despite being the living Word, He never did His own will but only the will of His Father (John 5:17–19; 8:28). And now, as a result of His submission, all other powers in the universe—visible and invisible—are submitted to Him, and all authority in heaven and earth is His (Matthew 28:18; Ephesians 1:19–22; Colossians 1:15–20; 1 Peter 3:22). This is the example we must follow, saying daily, "Lord, not my will, but Yours be done"—and that means radical submission. The results are worth it all.

You see, before we can say, "I must obey God rather than man"—I am speaking here primarily in the context of dealing with pressure to conform and compromise within the Body, not in the context of dealing with a Church-persecuting government—we must have a proven track record of submission to authority and of crucifying the flesh. Otherwise what we call obedience to God could simply be the manifestation of an unsubmitted, unaccountable, rebellious attitude.

As I wrote in 1991:

> What was radical yesterday is regular today. But someone had to break with the crowd. Someone had to step out—even if it meant being misunderstood by his own generation. Someone had to be bold and seem like a fool in the eyes of many in order to make a fresh move. How we need holy radicals in our day! (Let me insert a word of warning here: The most radical thing some of us could do is nail our self-will, arrogance and unsubmissiveness to the cross. Before God can fully use obnoxious mavericks He must first break them down.)[3]

And break them down He will. Otherwise they are of no use to His work. /

Really now, of what help are a large number of flakes? Of what value are mavericks beyond counting? Of what use are legions of unsubmitted troops?

Through many years of training college-age believers, I have seen this truth confirmed again and again: Those who do not welcome correction, those who are unwilling to humble themselves, those who will not submit to authority and those who fail to show respect to their elders will *not* make a lasting mark for God, nor will I pour myself into those kinds of people. The same applies to believers of all ages and walks of life, not just to young people: The Lord does not promote those with a lot of fleshly loose ends.

It is the attitude of heart that is vitally important, and a submitted heart carries much weight before the throne of God. It gets His attention and ultimately receives a substantial entrustment from heaven. A submitted heart can handle divine authority. But those who think their own frustration with "the system," be it the system of the world or the system of the Church, can fuel the revolution do not understand the ways of God. Flesh gives birth to flesh, and that is just as true in the twenty-first century as it was in the first. Yes, "God's righteousness doesn't grow from human anger" (James 1:20, MESSAGE), and a reactionary, self-righteous, unruly spirit will not produce holy fruit.

If we are to take a stand for truth even when others call us extremists; if we are to refuse unrighteousness even when pressured to compromise; if we are to call for radical change and swim against the tide even at great personal cost—we must be sure our motivations are not fleshly. If they are, we are simply rebels with a cause, manifesting our own independence.

Put another way, if you really want to be a Jesus revolutionary, you must crucify rebellion, independence, pride, self-will, ambition, anger, rage, retaliation and all related carnal behavior. You must cultivate humility, longsuffering and willingness to bear reproach; you must learn to turn the other cheek and overcome evil through good. The true Jesus revolutionary is a person whose flesh has been nailed to the cross. That is radical!

The plain fact is that almost every earthly revolution contains a strong element of rebellion against authority, and God hates rebellion.[4] In the Word rebellion is equated with divination (1 Samuel 15:23), and it was the hallmark of disobedient Israel. Again and again, God's sinning people were indicted as "a rebellious house" (see, for example, Isaiah 30:9; Ezekiel 2:5–8; Deuteronomy 31:27), and persistent rebellion is what brought Israel down.

Any rebellion in our lives must be uprooted ruthlessly, decisively and categorically. Rebellion is from the pit. It is a stiffening of the neck, a hardening of the heart, an obstinate determination to yield to self rather than to God. *It is antithetical to the Jesus revolution.* No rebels are welcome in His revolutionary army since, among other things, the Jesus revolution is a revolt against rebellion.

"Then how do we change the world?" you ask. "How do we break with dead tradition and bring about transformation? How do we act on the convictions that drive us day and night?"

The answer is simple: Through complete submission to the commands of Jesus, through total identification with His heart and through explicit obedience to His voice. We change the world by being like Jesus in character (who could be more effective than He was?) and being empowered with His Spirit for action (this certainly worked in the book of Acts!). We bring about transformation by carrying His burden, acting at His direction and executing His orders, rather than by getting aggravated and reacting in the flesh.

Consider the example of Moses. Perhaps he was already sensing his calling to liberate his people when he killed the Egyptian who was beating the Hebrew laborer. But it was not God's time and it certainly was not God's way, so Moses had to spend forty years on the backside of the desert before he was ready to set the captives free. Man's ways are not God's ways![5]

This means that when we say no to the system, it is not because we are simply fed up or frustrated or disillusioned or disturbed, but because we are saying yes to God. When we say to an authority figure, "I'm sorry, but I can't submit to your demands," it is not because we are unsubmissive to leaders but because we are totally submitted to the Father. As Watchman Nee explained:

> Submission is a matter of attitude, while obedience is a matter of conduct. Peter and John answered the Jewish religious council: "Whether it is right in the sight of God to hearken unto you rather than unto God, judge ye" (Acts 4:19). Their spirit was not rebellious, since they still submitted to those who were in authority. Obedience, however, cannot be absolute. Some authorities must be obeyed; while others should not be, especially in matters which touch upon Christian fundamentals— such as believing the Lord, preaching the gospel, and so forth. Children may make suggestions to their parents, yet they must not show an unsubmissive attitude. Submission ought to be absolute. Sometimes obedience is submission, whereas at other times an inability to obey may still be submission. Even when making a suggestion, we should maintain an attitude of submission.[6]

Yes, at certain times "an inability to obey may still be submission." That is a crucial concept. Nee continues:

> If parents should refuse to let their children gather with the saints, the children must maintain an attitude of submission though they may not necessarily obey. This is similar to the way the apostles responded to the Jewish council. When they were forbidden by the council to preach the gospel they kept a submissive spirit through-

91

out the trial; even so, they continued on with the Lord's commission. They did not disobey with quarrels and shoutings, they only quietly and softly dissented. There absolutely should neither be a word of slander nor an attitude of insubordination towards the governing authorities. One who knows authority will be soft and tender. He will be absolute in his submission both in his heart, in his attitude, and in his word. There will be no signs of harshness or rebellion.[7]

Is this becoming clearer? Obedience to Jesus does not give us the right to be haughty and rebellious, nor does it allow for unsubmissive attitudes of the heart. Right attitude will yield right action, especially when mixed with godly wisdom.

I am fully aware that many church leaders abuse their positions and wound their flocks, and that several key Scriptures have been taken out of context to keep leaders in power. I will address these problems in the coming chapters.

But right now our focus is on *our* hearts, *our* lives, *our* attitudes, *our* conduct. Are we really Jesus revolutionaries or are we merely self-righteous rebels who have found a spiritual outlet for our carnality? Are we truly fighting the Lord's battles, or are we using holy terminology as an excuse to air our grievances and carry out our agendas?

In 1 Peter, the Greek verb *hupatasso* (meaning "to submit") is used six times, once in the context of angels, authorities and powers being submitted to Jesus (1 Peter 3:22), and the other times in contexts related to our actions and attitudes: Believers are called to submit to all civil authorities for the Lord's sake (2:13–14); slaves are called to submit to their masters, even if those masters are cruel (2:18); wives are called to submit to their husbands, even if those husbands are not saved (3:1, 5); young men are called to submit to their elders (5:5).

Each of these contexts is different, and I do not believe God calls a woman to submit to her husband in the same way that a slave in the ancient world was called to submit to his master.[8] Nor do I believe that God's people are called to submit to a church leader in the same way a child is called to submit to a parent.[9] Yet, despite these different contexts, Peter uses the same word to describe the proper attitude toward authority. In other words a submitted person—be that person a Christian in society, a slave with a master, a wife with her husband or a young person with an elder—will act in submitted ways, because that is the attitude of the heart. Do you grasp this?

It is our submission to authority that empowers us to *disobey* authority in *obedience* to God. Listen again to Watchman Nee:

> When delegated authority (men who represent God's authority) and direct authority (God Himself) are in conflict, one can render submission but not obedience to the delegated authority. Let us summarize this under three points:
>
> Obedience is related to conduct: it is relative. Submission is related to heart attitude: it is absolute.
>
> God alone receives unqualified obedience without measure; any person lower than God can only receive qualified obedience.
>
> Should the delegated authority issue an order clearly contradicting God's command, he will be given submission but not obedience. We should submit to the person who has received delegated authority from God, but we should disobey the order which offends God.[10]

He offers the following examples from the Bible:

> The midwives and Moses' mother both disobeyed the decree of Pharaoh by preserving Moses alive. Yet they were considered to be women of faith.

The three friends of Daniel refused to bow to the golden image set up by King Nebuchadnezzar. They disobeyed the king's order, yet they submitted to the king's fire.

In disregard of the royal decree Daniel prayed to God; nevertheless he submitted to the king's judgment by being thrown into the lions' den.

Joseph took the Lord Jesus and fled to Egypt to avoid having the child killed by King Herod.

Peter preached the Gospel though it was against the command of the ruling council, for he said it was right to obey God rather than men. Yet he allowed himself to be taken into prison.[11]

/ In light of this, I prefer to speak of "biblical obedience" rather than "civil disobedience," since our primary calling is not so much disobedience to ungodly demands as it is obedience to God's commands. And so our call for revolution in the Church is not simply a call to go *against* what is wrong with the current system, but to go *with* the Spirit and the Word. We emphasize doing things God's way, not merely bringing about change.

It is interesting to contrast the philosophies of Mao Ze-dong—possibly the greatest mass murderer of the twentieth century, responsible for the deaths of as many as sixty million Chinese—and Mahatma Gandhi, who learned from Jesus the principle of nonviolent resistance, winning India's freedom from Britain with the loss of precious few lives.

As a boy Mao was constantly beaten and harassed by his domineering father—until he learned to fight back. Reflecting on an experience he had when he was thirteen, Mao related, "I learned that when I defended my rights by open rebellion my father relented, but when I remained meek and submissive he only cursed and beat me more."[12] So he chose open rebellion rather than meek submission, and as a result, oceans of innocent blood soaked his land. Gandhi's approach was totally different. He said, "A non-violent revolution is not a program of seizure of power. It is a program of transformation of relationships, ending in a peaceful transfer of power."[13] He taught that by nonviolent refusal to cooperate with injustice, the power of injustice is broken.

The Gandhi way (really, the Jesus way) challenges the flesh, but it results in liberation. In contrast, Mao's way (really, Satan's way) gives full vent to fleshly anger and resentment, but it results in oppression. Which path will we choose? Mao preached change through open rebellion. Gandhi preached change through meekness and noncooperation with evil. What kind of revolution will you have?

Let's learn from the Master, the most radical revolutionary who ever lived, the ultimate nonconformist, the fearless and confrontational Prophet, the only Man who never bowed the knee to anyone or anything other than God. "Take my yoke upon you," He says, "and learn from me, for I am gentle and humble in heart [or, in the classic language of the King James, *meek and lowly in heart*], and you will find rest for your souls" (Matthew 11:29 emphasis added). Gentleness and meekness are hallmarks of the Jesus way. *That* is revolutionary.

"Blessed are the meek," Jesus says, "for they will inherit the earth." Meekness is a major foundation of the Lord's upside-down Kingdom and a key to how the revolution is won. As the commentators explain: "And the meek—not the strong, aggressive, harsh, tyrannical—will inherit the earth."[14] Yes,

> The meek are those who quietly submit themselves to God, to his word and to his rod, who follow his directions, and comply with his designs, and are *gentle towards all men* (Tit. 3:2); who can bear provocation with-

out being inflamed by it; are either silent, or return a soft answer; and who can show their displeasure when there is occasion for it, without being transported into any indecencies; who can be cool when others are hot; and in their patience keep possession of their own souls, when they can scarcely keep possession of any thing else. *They* are the meek, who are rarely and hardly provoked, but quickly and easily pacified; and who would rather forgive twenty injuries than revenge one, having the rule of their own spirits.[15]

And while meekness does not always mean silence— Jesus, Paul and the apostles spoke up clearly and loudly when appropriate, exposing injustice, rebuking hypocrisy, telling their story to the world, declaring, "We will not comply!"—it always *does* mean crucifying reactionary behavior. And since God is the ultimate Ruler, working out everything according to His plan, doing His will His way produces His results. In the end it is the meek who will win.

This is what the Polish labor union leaders learned in defeating Communism:

One Friday night in December 1981, Lech Walesa and other leaders of Solidarity were arrested after a meeting in Gdansk. For sixteen months, their free trade union movement had shaken the foundation of communist power in Poland by occupying factories and staging strikes. Now martial law had been imposed, and Solidarity was looking down a gun barrel at defeat. But when he was [struck and] taken away, Walesa challenged his captors, "At this moment, you lost," he told them. "We are arrested, but you have driven a nail into your communist coffin. You'll come back to us on your knees."[16]

Did you hear that? "At this moment, you lost"—because you have used your power to oppress and attack those who will not fight back with violence. And Walesa was right. By not fighting force with force or intimidation with intimidation, the power of Communist rule was broken.

How contrary this is to the ways of the world! How contrary to a carnal revolutionary! How utterly maddening for the flesh! But if we want to advance the cause of Christ, the flesh must die—totally. Flesh and Spirit do not mix.

"Blessed are the poor in spirit," Jesus says, "for theirs is the kingdom of heaven." And in saying this, He shuts the door on self-reliance and pride. "Blessed are those who mourn, for they will be comforted." Yes, brokenness and tenderness of heart—not boasting or bigness—attract the response of the Father. And just as the Word teaches that "what is highly valued among men is detestable in God's sight" (Luke 16:15), so also what is often detestable among men is highly valued by the Lord. As the Scripture states:

> For this is what the high and lofty One says—
>     he who lives forever, whose name is holy:
> "I live in a high and holy place,
>     but also with him who is contrite and lowly in spirit,
> to revive the spirit of the lowly
>     and to revive the heart of the contrite."
>
> Isaiah 57:15

And again:

> He has showed you, O man, what is good.
>     And what does the LORD require of you?
> To act justly and to love mercy
>     and to walk humbly with your God.
>
> Micah 6:8

The humble attract His favor and receive His grace. But God resists the proud, and what God resists will soon desist.

Yes, a prideful spirit can also short-circuit the revolution. As Gordon Lindsay wrote concerning John Alexander Dowie, the dauntless and controversial pioneer of divine healing (1847–1907),

> No enemy could harm John Alexander Dowie, but the enemy within himself. Human pride, or tendency to self-exaltation, if given the least chance to assert itself, sets in motion an inexorable reverse law in the spiritual world—the law of spiritual gravitation, which ever works to bring the exalted low. As one rises higher and higher in spiritual power and blessing, and as his influence among men becomes greater and greater, then, as Dr. Dowie once said . . . he must ever seek to become lower and lower and lower.[17]

If you want to be lifted up by the Lord, get low. If you want to be an instrument in His hand, learn to submit. Otherwise your agenda will stall and you will find yourself stopped dead in your tracks. "Humble yourselves, therefore, under God's mighty hand, that he may lift you up in due time" (1 Peter 5:6). It can be very frustrating at times, but the end results are worth it. You will receive an ample supply of God's grace, and you will be lifted up at the proper time.

Let's deal strongly with pride in our lives, since a proud heart is a fertile breeding ground for a rebellious spirit.

Here are some potential evidences of pride (concentrate on examining yourself, rather than pointing the finger at others):

You are accountable to no one.

You think you are "the one"—that *your* church, *your* ministry, *your* anointing or *your* teaching is the necessary ingredient for true revival or evangelism or growth.

Your opinion is always more important than the opinion of others.

You are able to find sin in the lives of others but not in your own.

You are quarrelsome.

You find it difficult to be a team player.

You are always right about everything.

You are slow to repent.

You find it difficult to say, "I'm sorry," without defending yourself or blaming others.

You refuse to take help.

You are unteachable.

You are unable to recognize others' accomplishments or rejoice in their successes.

You are unable to say, "I'm hurting; I'm in trouble."

You never reverse your path when wrong, but make only minor adjustments.

You always think, "This message is for someone else, not me."

You fail to realize when God is trying to get your attention, when He is correcting you, when He is judging you.

I wince when I read a few of these; they hit me where it hurts. But even more than the conviction I feel is the confidence I have that He who began a good work in me will bring it to completion (see Philippians 1:6). This is His work, His revolution, His Church, His Body. We are His children, His workmanship, His ambassadors, His servants—and He is jealous for everything that bears His holy name.

If you and I submit ourselves to Him and resist the devil (see James 4:7), we *will* be vessels of honor. If we root out pride and rebellion, by the help of His Spirit, we *will* make an impact on this generation. We *will* be world changers and see His revolution sweep the land. Let us press on in His power! Now is not the time to falter or slow down.

Jesus revolutionaries hunger and thirst for righteousness; they are merciful and pure in heart. They are peacemakers who are persecuted for righteousness' sake and because of their identification with the Messiah. As a result they will be filled and they will obtain mercy; they will see God and be called His children. The Kingdom of heaven is theirs, and their heavenly reward will be rich.

This is the life God requires, the life He will bless—and we need His blessing if we are to see a revolution in the Church, let alone a revolution in the world. But with His blessing it will happen!

In the next three chapters we will be swimming in some treacherous waters, confronting abuses in "the system" and addressing the misuse of authority in the Church today. In such waters, only the humble and holy emerge unharmed.

Are you still coming along?

# 7

# Covering or Smothering?

(OR, HAS GOD ORDAINED PROTESTANT POPES?)

The pope can be judged by no one; the Roman church has never erred and never will err till the end of time; the Roman church was founded by Christ alone; the pope alone can depose and restore bishops; he alone can make new laws, set up new bishoprics, and divide old ones; he alone can translate [transfer] bishops; he alone can call general councils and authorize canon law; he alone can revise his judgments; his legates, even though in inferior orders, have precedence over all bishops; an appeal to the papal courts inhibits judgment by all inferior courts; a duly ordained pope is undoubtedly made a saint by the merits of St. Peter.

Pope Gregory VII, eleventh century
cited in Benson Bobrick,
*Wide as the Waters: The Story of the English Bible
and the Revolution It Inspired*

> For even if I boast somewhat freely about the authority the Lord gave us for building you up rather than pulling you down, I will not be ashamed of it. . . . This is why I write these things when I am absent, that when I come I may not have to be harsh in my use of authority—the authority the Lord gave me for building you up, not for tearing you down.
>
> 2 Corinthians 10:8; 13:10

*If you have not read chapter 6, "Revolutionary, Not 'Rebelutionary,'" don't continue reading! First study that chapter carefully, digest its contents and then continue here. If you absolutely refuse, you are showing signs of a wrong attitude!*

If it is true that rebellion is a dangerous, sinful attitude, then it follows that we should be extremely wary of calling a fellow believer rebellious. Yet Christian leaders fling such charges around freely, often branding godly, sensitive, gentle-hearted believers with the ugly title of *rebel,* saying of them almost flippantly—and with that all-knowing, condescending nod—"Oh, yes, he [or she] is in rebellion."

Why is such a serious charge made? Most of the time it is because the believer disagreed with the pastor in a matter of conscience or conviction or scriptural interpretation. And for something as small as that, he or she is labeled a rebel. How absurd!

On what basis are such charges made? Where does the New Testament ever require mindless submission and robot-like compliance to authorities within the Body? Who said that disagreement with a church leader constituted rebellion? (Please remember: I write this as a leader, not as a disgruntled, complaining parishioner.) What verse in the Bible states that it is wrong to raise fair and honest questions, with a meek and gracious spirit, to Christian leaders? How can this possibly be called rebellion? Yet it is, in churches across the land, leaving a path of bloodied, battered and bruised believers—the result of abusive spiritual authority.

Not only does this ministerial malpractice hurt the flock and grieve the heart of Jesus the Great Shepherd; it also stands in the way of spiritual progress, often preventing believers from moving forward in the Lord. At times it even competes with the Headship of Jesus over His Church, since His delegated authorities in the Body sometimes restrict His people from carrying out His will rather than empowering them to live it out.

Not surprisingly, when these sincere children of God try to follow the leading of His Spirit and walk in obedience to Him—which sometimes means differing with their leaders—they are called rebellious. What a travesty! Listening to the voice of Jesus, the Shepherd of the flock, is called rebellion by one of His undershepherds (who is a sheep himself). Thus obedience to God is viewed as disobedience to leadership, while submission to the authority of Jesus is branded resistance to church authority, and a healthy fear of the Lord is labeled pride and independence. No wonder so many believers are doing so little for God.

To be sure, at times spiritual stagnation is our fault alone. We need to get our own lives in order—turning from sin, getting serious with God, yielding to His will. It is our responsibility to walk in obedience, and ultimately there is no excuse for a believer's failure to fulfill God's will. But contributing factors do exist, and one of these is a constricting leadership style that leaves believers bound up, tied up and shut up by the very people who are supposed to help loose them and let them go.

Consequently these Christians not only suffer from the "audience" mentality, attending a weekly religious performance and paying their dues; they not only labor under the false mindset of "going to church" rather than "being the Church," thereby forgetting about their own calling and anointing to serve; but they are told to conform and submit without questioning anything, without searching the Scriptures for themselves and, above all, without discussion of any kind.

Lest anyone misunderstand me, I want to repeat once more how much I believe in proper submission to authority. I believe there is a terrible lack of respect for authority in our society today—in epidemic proportions—both inside and outside the Church. In fact, I believe this is such a serious problem that, for the first time in my life, after writing more than fifteen books, I put that warning at the beginning of this chapter, urging you to first read an earlier chapter that deals ruthlessly with rebellion and pride before reading these three chapters on the abuse of authority.

Getting rid of rebellion is very important to me. And as much as it lies with me, I will not contribute to a rebellious, independent attitude in the Church. Americans are notorious for a fleshly, independent spirit, and young people especially are prone to rebellion. As one who ministers extensively to American, college-age believers, I am very sensitive to these issues.

To repeat: A prideful, rebellious, independent, unsubmitted heart is a stench in God's nostrils, and He resists it vigorously. Of all the biblical terms for doing wrong, such as *sin, transgress* and *rebel,* the last one is the worst. But while the lack of submission to authority is a great problem in the Body today, the abuse of spiritual authority is also reaching a critical mass. In fact, I am convinced that in certain ways this unbiblical, stifling spiritual control is the *greater* problem right now, constituting one of the key areas in which a revolution in the Church is desperately needed.

Let me give you an all-too-typical example that will help illustrate just how destructive this controlling ministry mentality really is.

Let's say the pastor of a large, non-charismatic congregation begins to preach on the need for revival in the Church. Several months later, after much corporate prayer, God begins to pour out His Spirit on the hungry flock, and hundreds of lives are transformed. But the outpouring proves too intense for the pastor and his board, so they decide to shut down what God is doing and go back to their old, traditional ways.[1]

Not surprisingly, many in the church are unhappy, feeling that the Spirit has been quenched and a move of God thwarted. But when they seek to bring their concerns to the leadership—not in a harsh, combative way, but in a determined effort to seek and speak the truth rather than gossip about their leaders behind their backs—they are told that they just do not understand. In fact, they are told that they are operating in spiritual pride (although in the past they have been singled out as models of humility), that they have a problem with authority (although their record of service through the years has been exemplary) and that the recent outpouring served to reveal some junk in their own lives (although *during* the outpouring they were asked to testify to the great work the Spirit had accomplished in their lives). What in the world is going on?

But the story is not yet over for these hurting Christians. After months of deep inner conflict, much painful soul-searching and even bouts of self-condemnation ("Maybe I really am rebellious. Maybe I do have a problem with pride. Was I really touched by the Spirit? Maybe it was all just emotionalism."), they feel they should leave the church and join another local assembly that affirms the gifts and power of the Spirit. So they lovingly inform the leadership of their decision, asking to be released with blessing and thanking the leaders for everything they have done through the years. And what are they told in response? They are told they are in rebellion!

Soon enough, perhaps the very next Sunday, ominous threats are sounded from the pulpit, warning the startled hearers about "the rebellion," urging the congregants not to join this insidious, undermining movement, and reminding them of what God did to Korah and his followers when they tried to rebel against Moses: The earth opened its mouth and swallowed them up. So beware!

The pastor is now pulling out some of his vintage messages from Numbers and Deuteronomy in which the rebellious Israelites dared to disobey Moses, the servant of the Lord, falling in the wilderness as a result. It is time to warn the flock!

"Safety will only be found in staying here under the covering of the mother church. *This* is the place of protection. *This* is the place of security. Outside these walls lurk all kinds of deceptive spirits. Doctrinal purity and true church order are found *here*. And remember what happened to Miriam and Aaron when they dared to grumble about some of the decisions made by Moses: God rebuked them audibly, and Miriam was smitten with leprosy.

"And not only are you in danger; you are also being ungrateful and disloyal. After all, I'm the one who performed your weddings and conducted your families' funeral services. I was there for you during your times of trouble. My staff and my leaders have poured themselves out for you, putting you first, sacrificing time and energy and money, living such godly and holy lives—all for you!

"How then can you question those whom God has placed in authority over you? We love you and care for you, and the drastic measures we are taking today are being taken only for you. Just as a parent can't explain everything to a child, we can't explain everything to you. Just trust us, search your heart for a rebellious attitude and support your leadership now. This message is for *you.*"

Perhaps in the midst of these sermons, some prophetic utterances come forth, echoing the words of Psalm 105:15, "Touch not My anointed, and do My prophets no harm," with direct application to the present situation: "Don't you *dare* express any disagreement with these anointed servants of the Lord. God will not be happy with that!"[2]

What makes this story so sad is that it is not exaggerated. To the contrary, it is common, especially in evangelical circles (and possibly in Pentecostal and charismatic churches in particular, since one dare not question the charismatic leader). Yet such practices are both manipulative and abusive, using fear and guilt to dominate and control the flock.

How contrary this is to the shepherd's heart, and how utterly destructive and cruel, since it is *shepherds* who are wounding and mistreating the trusting *sheep.* Yet it has happened thousands of times. All this is contrary to the Word of God, as Scripture nowhere gives leaders this kind of authority over their people.

You might ask, "What about Hebrews 13:17? The Scripture says, 'Obey your leaders and submit to their authority. They keep watch over you as men who must give an account. Obey them so that their work will be a joy, not a burden, for that would be of no advantage to you.'[3] Doesn't that mean that I do whatever my leaders tell me to do, regardless of my conviction or opinion? Doesn't that mean that I follow their orders unless they tell me to violate the Scriptures? After all, the verse says, 'Obey and submit,' not, 'Think about it and comply only if you feel like it and agree.'"

I certainly agree that we should have a submissive attitude to authority, and that in many cases we obey spiritual leadership whether we like it or not.[4] What is in dispute is how much authority God gives to church leaders and to what extent they are called to direct the lives of His people.

For example, what if you were twenty years old and engaged to be married, and your pastor said to you, "You need to marry someone else. You're engaged to the wrong person, and I've picked out your spouse." Would you simply submit and obey? If not, what Scripture supports you? What verse in the Bible says, "Pastors cannot arrange marriages for their congregants," or, "Obey your leaders unless they tell you whom to marry"? Where is that written?

Or what if you were married and your pastor said to you, "I want you and your spouse to do your best to have twelve children"? Would you automatically say, "Well, the man of God told us to have twelve kids, so let's do our best to comply"? I seriously doubt it.

Now, you might say, "Hang on a minute. You're not being fair. It's outlandish to think that Christian leaders would confer that kind of authority on themselves." But that is really beside the point (although in some cult-like, controlling situations, examples such as this are not outlandish at all).[5] The point is simply this: Where is it written in the Bible that church leaders do *not* have that kind of authority? Who is to say they *cannot* order you to do such things?

If you say, "We're called to obey our leaders no matter what," that means you have to marry whom they tell you to marry, have as many kids as they tell you to have (or not have any kids if they say so), give as much money to the church as they tell you to give, live where they tell you to live and do whatever else they tell you to do—if they choose to make such demands.

You reply, "But God will protect me if they're wrong."

Says who? Why should God protect you or me if we fail to seek His face, fail to consult Him for His will, fail to use wisdom (or common sense!), fail to search the Scriptures for ourselves, fail to be responsible. Where is it written that if we simply submit to wrong counsel— no questions asked, no concerns raised—the Lord will bless us because we submitted?[6]

According to the Word of God every believer is a priest of the Most High God with direct access to His throne, and Jesus said that His sheep hear *His* voice (John 10:1–5, 27), Paul taught that all of God's children are led by His Spirit (Romans 8:14–16) and John wrote that the anointing resides in each of us (1 John 2:20). On what scriptural basis can we shirk our responsibility to hear the Lord for our own lives and simply obey whatever the authority demands, regardless of how extreme or absurd those demands may be?

Think back to some of the examples cited in the last chapter. Did the Hebrew midwives say, "Our authority, Pharaoh, has commanded us to kill all male children born to our people, so we will obey him and God will bless us for that"? No. They disobeyed the demands of the authority and God *blessed* them for *disobeying*— because Pharaoh, their authority, stepped outside of his rightful bounds and ordered them to sin.

"But now *you're* missing the point," you argue. "When our authorities tell us to disobey the written Word, we don't obey. For everything else we obey."[7]

109

I agree with the first half of this statement. But if that is the only time we can rightfully disobey, then, based on that logic, if your pastor tells you whom to marry, you *do* have to marry that person—and the Bible does not guarantee that God will bless you if you make the wrong choice. Also, as we saw in the last chapter, the Scriptures teach that when the voice of God is in conflict with the voice of man, even if that voice is the voice of an authority, we must obey God rather than man (always with a submitted attitude, always with proper respect shown toward the authority and always accepting the consequences of our choices).

You ask, "But what about 1 Peter 2:18? It is written there, 'Slaves, submit yourselves to your masters with all respect, not only to those who are good and considerate, but also to those who are harsh.'"

My friend, you are misusing the Word of God here. The pastor is not the master and the congregant is not the slave! In a master-slave relationship, the master *owned* the slave and had every legal right to work that slave to the bone. He was the absolute boss, and the slave lived to do his master's will. Obviously no Christian leader has any such rights over his congregants, and it is unacceptable that any pastor would try to use this verse to support his authoritarian rule over the flock. (To any believer enslaved in such an unscriptural church relationship, I recommend the counsel Paul had for slaves: "If you can gain your freedom, do so!"[8] In other words, get out as quickly as you can. Run for your life!)

Not only does the master-slave relationship not apply to believers in the Church, but when Peter dealt with the subject of submission to Church leadership (in the very same epistle), his counsel was quite different, addressing the elders first:

110

To the elders among you, I appeal as a fellow elder, a witness of Christ's sufferings and one who also will share in the glory to be revealed: Be shepherds of God's flock that is under your care, serving as overseers—not because you must, but because you are willing, as God wants you to be; not greedy for money, but eager to serve; not lording it over those entrusted to you, but being examples to the flock. And when the Chief Shepherd appears, you will receive the crown of glory that will never fade away.

1 Peter 5:1–4

Look at these directives: Don't be shepherds because you have to but because you want to; don't do it out of greed but out of eagerness to serve; don't lord it over the flock, but be an example.

That is how Peter describes Christian leadership, putting his emphasis on the leader's behavior more than on the believer's submission. Notice also that even Peter, the mighty apostle, gives an appeal rather than makes a demand. He is sensitive to the issue of domineering over the flock. Only after appealing to the elders does he write, "Young men, in the same way be submissive to those who are older," closing with this amazing exhortation: "All of you, clothe yourselves with humility toward one another, because, 'God opposes the proud but gives grace to the humble'" (1 Peter 5:5). All must get low before the Lord.

This is incredible! He does not tell the younger believers to submit to their elders as a slave submits to his master or a Roman citizen submits to the king.[9] Rather he puts the onus on the conduct of the elders, who are called to serve more than they are called to rule. And he calls for young men to follow the example of their elders, something he did not say about masters and slaves, because (as I said) the pastor of a church is not

111

the master and the congregants are not the slaves. It is that simple.

As New Testament scholar Peter Davids observed (commenting on 1 Peter 5:3):

> Jesus had clearly pointed out that the way of [the] world at large was for leaders to domineer over the led, expecting obedience and the "perks" of leadership. But that was not to be the model his disciples were to follow (Mark 10:42). His disciples were to be servants, not bosses; ministers, not executives.[10] /

That really says it all.

We can make the following statements, then, without any fear of scriptural contradiction, although I am sure some leaders will be upset with me for putting this in writing, fearing that it will undermine their authority. Sorry! Truth is truth, and just as God does not appreciate lack of submission to His authority, He does not appreciate the usurping of His authority. And to my fellow leaders I say this: If the following statements threaten your ability to lead, you have some serious soul-searching to do.

According to the Word of God:

- The pastor is not the king.
- The pastor is not the pope.
- The pastor is not the Lord.
- The pastor is not the sovereign ruler.
- The pastor is not the infallible guide.
- The pastor is not the general of the Army (or the admiral of the Navy).
- The pastor is not the CEO of the company.
- The pastor *is* (ideally) one key part of a team of leaders whose primary calling is to serve.

Tom Marshall, a Christian leader from New Zealand, set some excellent parameters for spiritual authority, quoting from the writings of Menno Simons, one of the founders of the Mennonite Church. As Marshall points out, the quote is especially remarkable since it comes from the Reformation era, "a time when theological opponents were generally burned at the stake." Simons wrote:

> Spiritual authority is never to make the rebel conform; its only purpose is to enable the obedient person to live a holy life. Therefore it rests on submission and obedience freely given. Furthermore, spiritual authority has only spiritual means at its disposal; its only weapons are prayer, scripture, counsel and the power of a holy life.[11]

Marshall's own observations are extremely important as well:

> Church leaders who are exercising spiritual authority must therefore strenuously avoid coercion and manipulation in any form whatsoever, whether by force of will or personality, charisma or reputation, or group or peer pressure. Even more to be shunned are claims to divine revelation or divine sanction to back up directives or reinforce views or opinions. . . . You cannot be another person's conscience and you cannot be God to him or her.[12]

This approach to leadership and authority is radically different from the approach many of us have been exposed to, and I am sure some readers will think, *This guy is completely doing away with the whole authority structure of the church.* Hardly! I am merely seeking to distinguish the Jesus pattern of leading from the worldly, abusive pattern of leading.

As one who has been involved in traveling ministry for nearly twenty years, I help prepare workers who are

113

getting ready for itinerant preaching. And one of the key areas we discuss deals with their submission to the authority of the local church.

Without exception I tell them that if they feel led to give an altar call at the end of their message but the pastor tells them not to, they are to submit to the pastor's authority, even if they feel that souls are hanging in the balance. It is permissible for them to ask the leader to reconsider, but his word must be taken as final, and they are not to grumble or complain or show a disrespectful attitude.[13]

This applies to any visiting minister, regardless of age or experience. You are on someone else's turf, and you must play by the rules of that house. If you cannot play by those rules, you can choose not to return in the future. In a severe case of conflict, you and the pastor might even agree to cancel any remaining meetings. But under no circumstances should you overrule the local authorities because you feel the Spirit's prompting. If you have a word of protest, make it known to those authorities, urging them lovingly to reconsider. You have then discharged your duty, and the responsibility is now theirs.

I see this as simple, scriptural common sense: You must play by the rules of the house. But I also see something else that is equally simple, scriptural and clear: If you disagree with the rules of the house, you can leave the house!

No minister or church owns you, and no one has the right to tell you that your convictions are not from the Lord unless those convictions are contrary to the Scriptures. In light of this, I find it interesting that many church leaders turn this upside down. They tell their congregants, "You must submit to everything I say unless it runs contrary to the Scriptures," rather than, "You must hold fast to your convictions before the Lord

114

unless those convictions run contrary to the Word." There is quite a difference!

Once again Tom Marshall has something important to say on this, emphasizing that spiritual authority "is concerned with character and character change," and because of this,

> spiritual authority must be deeply committed to . . . [the] integrity of moral choice, and therefore the necessity for people to decide and make choices on the basis of conscience. In fact, in moral or spiritual issues, if a person is not deciding on the basis of conscience they are not acting morally at all, they are acting non-morally.[14]

How this flies in the face of the typical, heavy-handed leadership! It reminds us that every believer is ultimately accountable to Jesus, the Head of the Body and Lord of the Church. Therefore, when a leader demands that a believer go against his or her conscience he is asking that believer to act in a non-moral way. This is a serious issue. And while it is true that leaders are accountable to God for their care of the flock (see again Hebrews 13:17, quoted above), it is also true that in the New Testament believers are never told they are "accountable" to their leaders. Our primary accountability is to God.[15]

Again, this is not to say that leaders are not to lead; neither is it to say that leaders do not have authority; nor is it to say that believers are not called to submit to the authority of their leaders. It is to say that: (1) Leaders have authority to build up, edify, teach, train, correct, rebuke, encourage, equip, shepherd and guide, but *not* to tear down, domineer, control, manipulate and tyrannize; (2) we are called to *willingly place ourselves under spiritual authority*, which is different from leaders demanding submission from their flocks; (3) leaders do not have authority outside of the Lord. In other words, if a leader rejects the will of God in favor of his own will, he can no longer make claim to his God-given authority.

Watchman Nee pointed this out in his oft-quoted book *Spiritual Authority*. He stated that there are three requirements for delegated authority, the first of which is that

> *He must know that all authority comes from God.* Every person who is called to be a delegated authority should remember that "there is no authority except from God; and those that exist are set up by God" (Rom. 13:1). He himself is not the authority, nor can anyone make of himself an authority. His opinions, ideas, and thoughts are no better than those of others. They are utterly worthless. Only what comes from God constitutes authority and commands man's obedience. A delegated authority is to represent God's authority, never to assume that he too has authority.[16]

Did you grasp that? The leader himself does not have authority. "Only what comes from God constitutes authority and commands man's obedience." As Nee explains,

> The policeman and the judge execute authority and enforce the law, but they should not write the law themselves. Likewise, those who are placed in authority in the church merely represent God's authority.[17]

It is easy to lose sight of this, since power and authority can easily go to a person's head, be that person a policeman or a pastor, and he or she can forget that his or her role is not to write new laws but rather to enforce existing laws.

> For one to be in authority does not depend on his having ideas and thoughts; rather does it hinge on knowing

116

the will of God. The measure of one's knowledge of God's will is the measure of his delegated authority. God establishes a person to be His delegated authority entirely on the basis of that person's knowledge of God's will. It has nothing at all to do with having many ideas, strong opinions, or noble thoughts. Indeed, such persons who are strong in themselves are greatly to be feared in the church.[18]

What a striking statement! "Such persons who are strong in themselves are greatly to be feared in the church." Why? Because they will rely on their own abilities or charisma or persuasiveness rather than on God's will and anointing, ruling by the power of the flesh instead of the power of the Spirit. Yet a leader's primary purpose is to bring people into a deeper knowledge of God and greater usefulness in His Kingdom. Leaders are not raised up to fulfill their visions or build their kingdoms or draw disciples after themselves (see Acts 20:28–31) but rather to draw people after the Lord. As Nee explains:

> Many young brothers and sisters are as yet unlearned, not knowing God's will; hence God has put them under authority. Those in authority are responsible to instruct these younger ones in the knowledge of God's will. However, in each and every dealing with them, it is imperative for the delegated authority to know beyond doubt what the Lord's will is in that particular affair. Then he may act as God's representative and minister with authority. Apart from such knowledge, he has no authority to command obedience.[19]

Once again, I interrupt these words to emphasize the point being made: If the leader does not know with certainty the will of God, "he has no authority to command obedience," since he can only call for obedience

117

to God's will, not his will. Remember: The leader is *God's delegated authority*—and this carries a high level of responsibility.

> No one is able to be God's delegated authority unless he has learned to obey God's authority and understand His will. To illustrate. If a man represents a certain company in negotiating a business contract, before he signs the contract he must first consult with his general manager; he cannot sign the agreement independently. Similarly, one who acts as God's delegated authority needs to first know the will and the way of God before he is able to put authority into effect. He can never give to the brothers and sisters an order which God has not given. Were he to tell others what to do and yet not have it acknowledged by God, he would be representing himself and not God. Hence it is required of him that he first know God's will before he acts on God's behalf. Then shall his action come under God's approval. Only God's acknowledged judgment is authoritative; whatever comes from man is wholly void of authority, for it can only represent himself.[20]

This is one of the great tragedies of abusive spiritual authority: At times leaders will hatch their own carnal plan (often under financial pressure) rather than do things God's way, seeking to enforce it by means of their position as leaders, even pressuring the flock for funds in order to make their plan work. "Remember," they say, "we are your leaders, appointed by God, so you must give yourselves wholeheartedly to our vision"—but everyone with eyes to see can recognize that they are acting in the flesh. Yet no one is allowed to question them or disagree, since they are the anointed leaders. Anyone who does question them is in rebellion against the Lord. What a *misuse* of authority this is!

Nee therefore rightly says:

For this reason we must learn to rise high and touch deeply in spiritual things. We need to have a more abundant knowledge of God's will and way. We should see what others have not seen and attain to what others have not attained. What we do must come from what we have learned before God, and what we say must issue from that which we have experienced of Him. There is no authority except God. If we have seen nothing before God, then we have absolutely no authority before men. All authority depends on what we have learned and known before God. Do not think that because one is older he can suppress the younger, because one is a brother he can oppress the sisters, or because one is quick-tempered he can subdue the slow in temper. To try to do this will not be successful. Whoever wishes that others be subject to authority must himself first learn to know God's authority.[21]

"But," you ask, "doesn't this approach compromise one's authority as a leader?"

Not at all! If you are truly called by God to your position, if you have a proven track record, and if you have served the flock and are known by your people (that means having relationships), they will submit joyfully and sacrificially. As a leader in the Body, I have witnessed this for years, and those to whom we have ministered are incredibly loyal, incredibly devoted, incredibly submitted, incredibly faithful. It is because the authority is both earned (by service and relationship) and recognized (by anointing and track record).

Year in and year out I see people pledge their lives for the work, for the other leaders and for me—willingly, joyfully, without coercion—yet we are never domineering, we never abuse those "under" us, and we never threaten people or force them to submit. This kind of authority is heavenly and relational. In contrast, the "royal pastor" model *downgrades* the heavenly by mixing it with fleshly coercion and *denies* the relational by remaining aloof from the people, thereby *decreasing* rather than *increasing* spiritual authority.

As Jesus taught His power-hungry disciples:

> "You know that the rulers of the Gentiles lord it over them, and their high officials exercise authority over them. Not so with you. Instead, whoever wants to become great among you must be your servant, and whoever wants to be first must be your slave—just as the Son of Man did not come to be served, but to serve, and to give his life as a ransom for many."
>
> Matthew 20:25–28

> "In this world the kings and great men order their people around, and yet they are called 'friends of the people.' But among you, those who are the greatest should take the lowest rank, and the leader should be like a servant. Normally the master sits at the table and is served by his servants. But not here! For I am your servant."
>
> Luke 22:25–27, NLT[22]

Listen again to Peter Davids:

> Rather than dominating his house church, then, the elder is to lead by example: "being examples to the flock." This concept of leadership is common in the NT. Jesus often presented himself as an example (Matt. 10:24–25; Mark 10:42–45; Luke 6:40; John 13:16; 15:20). Paul could write, "Walk according to the example you had in us" (Phil. 3:17) and "We gave an example to you so that you might imitate us" (2 Thess. 3:9), or even "Be imitators of me, as I am of Christ" (1 Cor. 11:1; cf. Acts 20:35). Other leaders were also expected to be examples (1 Thess. 1:6–7; 1 Tim. 4:12; Tit. 2:7; Jas. 3:1–2). In fact, one could well argue that, following the pattern of the ancient world and especially Judaism, teaching and lead-

ing was for the NT basically a matter of example rather than of lecture or command. Being an example fits well with the image of "flock," for the ancient shepherd did not drive his sheep, but walked in front of them and called them to follow.[23]

The Jesus pattern turns everything upside down, reversing the example of the world, finding greatness in service and power in humility. God's Kingdom operates on different principles, and the spiritual revolution that we so desperately need calls for a radical reevaluation of leadership patterns based on Kingdom values.

Are those values challenging to the flesh? Absolutely. Are they a threat to the religious establishment? More than any of us realize. But don't stop reading now. We are about to rattle some cages, rock some boats, ruffle some feathers and upset some apple carts. Turn the page and see!

# 8

# Confronting
# the Pastoral Fraternity

(OR, HOW TO DISARM
THE MINISTERIAL LABOR UNION)

The whole history of the Church is one long story of this tendency to settle down on this earth and to become conformed to this world, to find acceptance and popularity here and to eliminate the element of conflict and of pilgrimage. . . . You are up against the trend of things religiously [as a pioneer]. See again this letter to the Hebrews. The trend was backward and downward toward the earth, to make of Christianity an earthly religious system, with all its externalities, its forms, its rites, its ritual, its vestments; something here to be seen and to answer to the senses . . . it made a great appeal to their souls, their natures, and the letter is written to say, "Let us leave these things and go on." We are pilgrims, we are strangers, it is the heavenly that matters. . . .

But it is a costly and a suffering thing to come up against the religious system that has "settled down" here. It is . . . far more costly than coming up against the naked world itself. The religious system can be more ruthless and cruel and bitter; it can be actuated by all those mean things, contemptible things, prejudices and suspicions, that you will not even find in decent people in the world. It is costly to go on to the heavenlies, it is painful; but it is the way of the pioneer, and it has to be settled that that is how it is. The phrase in this letter is, "Let us therefore go forth unto Him without the camp" (Heb.13:13), [which] means ostracism, suspicion. . . .

T. Austin Sparks, *Pioneers*

The institutional church in the next twenty years will continue more and more to look like the pink Cadillac with the huge tail fins.

Anonymous quote
cited in Leonard Sweet, *Post-Modern Pilgrims* (2000)

 *If you have not read chapter 6, "Revolutionary, Not 'Rebelutionary,'" don't continue reading! First study that chapter carefully, digest its contents and then continue here. If you absolutely refuse, you are showing signs of a wrong attitude!*

Pastors are some of the most underpaid, overworked and underappreciated people in our society. They are expected to be master of all trades, always anointed and always ready, professional and personal at the same time, there to marry the lovebirds, counsel the former lovebirds, visit the hurting, pray for the dying, bury the dead (or, in some circles, try to raise the dead), preach with passion, teach with wisdom, be serious yet funny, administratively excellent yet totally spontaneous, deep but easy to follow, heavenly yet earthly, separated yet accessible.

Pastors are expected to make the 2 A.M. emergency call at the hospital, the 6 A.M. prayer meeting at the church, the men's breakfast at 8 A.M., the staff meeting at 9 A.M., then be ready to bring the house down with a fiery sermon at 10 A.M. When all that is done, they need to talk with disgruntled parishioners until the doors close, eat lunch with visiting friends until late afternoon and return to bring a motivational message at 6 P.M. What a life!

If the pastor is ruled by the board (did you ever hear of a church being "deacon possessed"?), he's a spineless wimp; if he's unmoved by opinion, he's an autocratic tyrant. If he's a team player, he's indecisive; if he leads alone, he's full of himself. Isn't this how we view things?

If the air conditioning in the church building is not working, it's the pastor's fault. When it *is* working, well, that's just the way it should be. Who notices *that?* If the worship is too long (or too short or too loud or too soft or too outdated or too modern), it's the pastor's fault. When everyone is happy, it's the worship leader who is wonderful. If the pastor preaches to the saved, he's neglecting the lost; if he preaches to the lost—"Hey, we hired a pastor, not an evangelist!"

Even in the best-case scenario, the pastor faces the challenge of pleasing God and not people, while remaining sensitive to the needs of the flock; of staying on the cutting edge of what the Spirit is doing, while building stability into the church; of being trusting and transparent, while avoiding wolves who come clothed like sheep; of stewarding God's funds, while steering clear of exploitation and greed. And he is always in danger of negative comparisons to the last pastor ("What a man of God he was!") or the latest TV superstar preacher ("Wow! What a show!") or even the most recent guest speaker ("How anointed!").

Then there is the intense spiritual warfare that pastors and their spouses endure as they battle on the front lines and seek to make headway against hell. Along with this is the ongoing challenge of keeping up their own devotional lives in the midst of nonstop ministry busyness and the pressure of carrying the burdens of scores, if not hundreds or even thousands, of people.

Just think of some of the most difficult seasons in your life—perhaps a time of terrible tragedy or loss, or watching a loved one waste away with a debilitating illness—and then imagine being hit with *several of these crises a week,* not to mention being expected to have a word of comfort, a prayer of courage and a smile of confidence that will still the storm. That is what we expect of the contemporary pastor.

For all that, most pastors are grossly underpaid for the hours they put in, often facing retirement, weary and worn out, with very little in the way of benefits, housing or pension. This satirical want ad by one church says it all:

Wanted: the perfect pastor. Approximately 28 years old, with 30 years' preaching experience. Must have a heart for the youth, work well with the elderly, participate in church sports, visit every hospitalized member. Need top-flight negotiating skills, good singing voice, and expertise in repair of office equipment, church van, and fellowship hall plumbing. Office hours 7 a.m. till 10 p.m. Salary $100 per week. Will preferably tithe $50 per week, wear fashionable suits, have a large library. Must participate in evangelism outreaches, make 30 calls per day

125

on church members, always be in the office when parishioners phone. Walking on water a plus.[1]

Reading this, you hardly know whether to laugh or cry. There is a lot of truth to the exaggerated expectations expressed in this impossible ad!

I have great admiration for many of these servants of God who have given themselves to His work out of love for the Savior, love for His sheep and love for lost souls. The last thing I want to do is breed criticism or resentment toward my colleagues in pastoral ministry, and I urge you—I am speaking to the congregants, not the pastors, right now—to be a blessing and not a burden to your leaders; to serve and support them as much as you can without violating your own convictions; to build them up and not tear them down; to honor them and pray for them and recognize them. Find out how you can make their load lighter. Encourage, don't criticize; learn to smile, not scowl.

In the great majority of cases, these men and women of God are doing the best they know how to do, and even if their mindsets need adjusting and their methods need changing, this is probably the way they learned to do ministry in their home churches, or from their former pastors, or in Bible school or seminary, or through books and conferences, and it is probably the only way they understand. Don't fall into harsh judgment of your leaders. Judgmental attitudes do not please the Lord.

Having said that, I must say that all is not well in "Ministry Land." Some serious problems must be addressed, and I speak now to leaders and congregants alike. Fellow leaders, if what I am about to share is the truth, then join me in dismantling what can rightly be described as the ministerial labor union. Fellow believers, if what I am about to say is from the Lord, encourage your leaders to stand up against the politically correct system that I call the pastoral fraternity. If your leaders know that you support them, it will help them to stand up for the Kingdom of God at any cost.

But let me reiterate: I am a friend, not a foe, of pastors around the world, and if my words hurt it is because they are the faithful wounds of a friend (see Proverbs 27:5–6). I write not out of malice or resentment or anger. God forbid! He knows my heart all too well in this matter. Some of my best friends are senior pastors, and everything I do in ministry, Stateside or abroad, I do in conjunction with local pastors and leaders, which is all the more reason that these issues must be addressed.

What I write here I write out of the inescapable conviction that something is wrong with "the system"; that taking hold of the truths I am about to share will bring liberty and clarity rather than bondage and confusion; that the Kingdom pattern is the best pattern of all; that there *is* a better way; that it is time to make progress.

The pastoral fraternity stands in the way of this progress and hinders a fresh move of the Spirit. It is a system of spiritual territorialism, religious politics, and protection of position, often based on a leadership attitude of "You scratch my back, I'll scratch yours." It is *not* the Jesus way.

Interestingly, when I have addressed these very issues in leadership meetings in America and abroad, the leaders in attendance, mainly pastors, have urged me on, expressing their agreement. After I spoke on this at a major conference in Mexico, the nationally respected pastor who hosted the conference said to me, "Mike, you should have been even stronger. These guys [some of the local pastors] are like the Mafia!" How telling! I am not the only one to see that the emperor is not wearing any clothes.

Years ago I noticed a curious phenomenon. I was preaching around the world, and God was opening up significant doors of ministry opportunity. My books were being translated into a number of foreign languages, and wherever I traveled (especially in the States), people told me about the impact the books made on their lives. But when I visited a ministers' fellowship in my hometown, I discovered I was somewhat of a non-person in their eyes. Why? I was not part of the pastoral fraternity.

Even though the attendance was light and not all the men knew each other, the general feeling was clear. When they went around the room and introduced themselves, two key validating elements emerged: They could claim the title *pastor* and they had a church name behind them. To be involved in itinerant ministry was almost suspect. At the least it did not provide entrance into the inner circle.

I remember thinking to myself, If I simply put up a sign in front of my house that said "Pastor Michael Brown, Church of the King," and three people showed up for meetings, I would be one of the boys. Without being a pastor, I could not be part of the club.

This perception had nothing to do with my being a stranger to the other men, since I was known to a good number of them, while others were meeting each other for the first time. The problem was the fraternity mentality that prevailed. I have seen it time and time again, and not on the local level only. This fraternity can extend worldwide in the form of political alliances, even when no true relationships have existed in the past. This is similar to what happened when both Herod and Pilate condemned Jesus to death. On that day, Luke records, they "became friends—before this they had been enemies" (Luke 23:12).

The pastoral fraternity works like this: Pastor Smith and Pastor Jones have been cool toward each other through the years, never meeting together, never praying together, never participating in joint services, even though they are part of the same denomination and live in the same city. They view each other as competitors, and both find the other somewhat suspect in terms of character and practice.

But then Pastor Smith has a problem with Pastor James, a local leader from another denomination, and before you know it Pastor Smith and Pastor Jones are having lunch together, planning how to close ranks against Pastor James. The sad thing is that both of them know exactly what they are doing, yet neither brings up their past stormy relationship, nor does Pastor Jones care to pursue the truth about Pastor James and find out who is really right or wrong. Political alliances come first.

In an atmosphere like this, how can God's Kingdom advance? When human interests come before the cause of Jesus, how can the Spirit move? Where is the ministerial integrity? Where is the commitment to speak the truth in love? Where is the confrontation of wrong? Sadly, once a pastor becomes established in his ministry, he can become untouchable, even to the point of living in sin. (I know of some leaders who have fathered several children with several different women, but no one was willing to call them to account.) How can this be?

It is one thing to honor a spiritual father; it is another thing to compromise. It is one thing to recognize the elders of a city; it is another thing to play political games. Yet it is common for the senior city leaders to show solidarity with one another for their common good (remembering past "favors" done for them) while failing to show solidarity in confronting one another over issues of sin. And to think that we are called to be a holy people and a kingdom of priests!

Now, before anyone thinks I am being unfair or writing with a critical spirit, I want to reiterate my support for local churches and local church leaders. For years I have scheduled special meetings, whenever possible, for local leaders in every city in which I minister. And it is rare that I accept an invitation to minister in a region when the invitation does not come from local pastors. I affirm and honor the local church; that is why I am sticking my neck out by addressing these issues.

Love compels me to speak, and I encourage you to keep an open heart. In a moment I will propose a biblical approach to the problems at hand. But we must understand what is wrong before we can set things right. So I will stick my neck out even more and expose this glaring fault in the ministry—although I must say that leaders in the Body of Christ have been some of the strongest supporters of the message of this chapter, urging me to get it in print.

The pastoral fraternity is reminiscent of labor unions. I am sure that such unions do a lot of good and that a lot of fine people are involved in them. But what is the primary purpose of a union? Is it to improve the quality of the product for which the union is responsible? Not at all. Nor is it to find the most efficient and cost-effective way to do the work for those paying the bills. Rather, the primary purpose of a union is to ensure the well-being and prosperity of the union members. It is to protect their rights. And doing this preserves solidarity within the union ranks.

Most of us have witnessed comical situations in which five people making fifteen dollars an hour are needed to carry out some simple task that could easily be done by two people making minimum wage. What is the explanation? "It's union work!" And union workers protect one another, knowing that keeping the union strong is always in their best interests.

One of my friends coordinated a major Christian event in one of the largest auditoriums in the country.

Everything in this auditorium was union. If you were not union, you could not even move a plant or re-arrange the chairs. (I kid you not.) In other cities where we had conducted similar events, volunteers could do much of the work for free. Not here. This was a union operation from top to bottom—and that did not nec-essarily mean it was more efficient. To the contrary, some simple jobs took much longer to perform since we had to wait for the union workers to arrive and fol-low union guidelines.

But there was no bucking the system. Not a chance! If you wanted anything done, you had to play by the union's rules and pay them their wages. Period. The words *but there's a better way* never got spoken. Why? Because those words undermined the union. If you could find a more efficient way to get the job done, that would expose the inefficiency of the union approach, since unions exist to protect the workers' rights, not the customers' rights—so much like the pastoral fraternity! The comparison to labor unions is all too appropriate. (Did it suddenly get hot in the room?)

Here is a typical scenario. Suppose some of the pas-tors in a community become spiritually complacent. Out of love for His Church and love for the lost, God sends in some fresh blood from the outside. Now there is a new church plant in town, and soon sinners are being converted, backsliders are returning to the Lord and the sick are being healed. The Kingdom of God is advanc-ing. What wonderful news!

Alas, that is not the reaction from the pastoral fra-ternity. This newcomer is making them look bad. He is getting results following the Word of God, and the Spirit is backing him up. Plus his passion is exposing the luke-warmness of the "good old boys," who are none too keen to greet him when he starts attending the local pastors' fellowship. Why? Because this God-sent servant is now perceived as a threat. He has invaded their turf and, worst of all, met with success.

He also now understands why most of these men were cold to him when he first visited their meeting several months ago, sharing the exciting news that his denomination was sending him to plant a new work in their area. They did not want the competition![2] And so now, even when he assures them he does not want their sheep, that he is there to help them in any way possible, that he has no desire to make them look bad, that he is open to their counsel, they still look at him with distrust— *especially* when some of their people start attending meetings at the new church.

These pastors have forgotten that more than three-quarters of their own congregations consist of members of other churches. They have forgotten that when they first came to town, they welcomed with open arms disgruntled and hurting believers from other local assemblies, freely listening to their horror stories about the terrible things their old pastors did. "I'm so sorry to hear that," they said with compassion. "You'll not find any of that here. You'll find a shepherd who cares for the sheep. I can see why God sent me here to start a church! So many of you have been hurt by the ministry."

But now, when the shoe is on the other foot, when the new pastor is hearing horror stories about *them* and thinking to himself, *I can see why God sent me here to start a church,* he is rejected by many of the local leaders.

How does Jesus feel about this state of affairs? These are His sheep! This is His Kingdom! This is His harvest! Yet some of His servants are fighting over position and influence and power and control and people (which, by the way, also mean money). How carnal.

None of us died to redeem the lost. None of us has any ownership of the sheep. None of us has our own kingdom to build. We are here to do His work, and His work alone. Yet the labor union mentality can stifle it all, since the primary question is not "How can we best fulfill the Great Commission?" as much as it is "How does this affect my status, my security, my rights, my reputation, my work, my wages?"

It is one thing for a leader to take Paul's charge in Acts 20:28 seriously: "Keep watch over yourselves and all the flock of which the Holy Spirit has made you overseers. Be shepherds of the church of God, which he bought with his own blood." Jealousy for the flock's well-being is good. Watchfulness is healthy and necessary. But what is it that motivates the decisions of some leaders—a shepherd's heart or a selfish heart? (God alone is the judge.) And are newcomers rejected because they are a danger to the flock or because they are a danger to the union? We need to address these issues before the Lord.

When an established leader in the community falls into sin, are the other local leaders willing to confront their fallen colleague in love, or do they remember the special treatment he gave them in years past and look the other way? Is the solidarity with the fraternity or with the Lord? Is the focus on the flock's well-being or on the union leader's well-being?

Let me state clearly that I believe strongly in the concept of the church of the city—that God sees one church in every location, consisting of all believers in all the local assemblies—and that the leaders of these churches should work together in mutual honor, respect and solidarity.[3] I also believe that spiritual fathers should be esteemed, that sheep-stealing is a serious offense to God, and that those preaching heretical doctrine should be confronted and, if necessary, marked.

My issue has to do with ethics and integrity and biblical principles. It has to do with the wrongness of political alliances and siding with those in position rather than siding with truth. It has to do with the territorial mindset, which is antithetical to the Kingdom of God mentality.[4]

The plain fact is, it is time to dismantle the ministerial labor union. Here are several strategies—none of them new—that will pave the way for far more effective ministry.

1. Find deep personal security in Jesus. When you know who you are in Him, especially in terms of your calling, and when you have His affirmation and favor, you will not be moved by human opinion. Knowing He is pleased with you and that you are doing His will is more than enough compensation. Secure in Him, you will find yourself empowered to take courageous stands, to go against the grain of popular opinion, to speak the truth in love without worrying about the consequences. This is because you will be driven by the question "Does this please the Lord?" rather than "How will this play out? What will the people think? What will the brothers say?"

The fraternity/union mentality is primarily horizontal in nature, as leaders look to leaders for affirmation, self-worth and support. The biblical mentality is primarily vertical in nature, as the undershepherd looks to the Chief Shepherd for guidance, strength and confirmation. You will ultimately choose only one of these ways.

2. Smash carnal, political alliances and instead build godly friendships. Superficial relationships that exist mainly for the public eye will not defeat the powers of darkness, and the back-slapping, "good old boy" syndrome will not produce any true fellowship. Kingdom relationships require vulnerability, honesty, mutual sacrifice and the crossing of political (often equal to denominational) lines. Who will be the first to step out?

I have seen ministers use one another as long as it benefits their purposes. Then, when the partnership is no longer useful, the relationship is discarded like a hot potato. No more of this in Jesus' name!

3. Learn the power of team ministry. There is a reason *elders* and *leaders* are always mentioned in the plural in the New Testament. There is a reason that Peter and John ministered together, that Paul and Barnabas (then Paul and Silas) ministered together, that the book of Acts does not feature just "one big man."[5] There is a reason the Scriptures state:

> Two are better than one,
>> because they have a good return for their work:
> If one falls down,
>> his friend can help him up.
> But pity the man who falls
>> and has no one to help him up!
> Also, if two lie down together, they will keep warm.
>> But how can one keep warm alone?
> Though one may be overpowered,
>> two can defend themselves.
> A cord of three strands is not quickly broken.

>> Ecclesiastes 4:9–12

Now, this is not to deny the principle that "whenever God wants to do a work, He chooses a person."[6] I wholeheartedly affirm this as scriptural and practical, as well as historically true. Team ministry, however, does not negate individual calling. When properly carried out, it enhances individual gifts and strengths, just as a baseball pitcher's skills are enhanced by a good defensive team, and his winning percentage increases when he is backed by good hitters.[7] A ministry team consists of called individuals, and one of those individuals will also be called to lead the team.

Have you ever meditated on the meaning of Acts 2:14, which states that, after the outpouring at Pentecost, "Peter stood up *with the Eleven*, raised his voice and addressed the crowd" (emphasis added)? When Peter stood, they all stood with him.[8] His voice was their voice, his words their words. Thus he proclaimed, "God has raised this Jesus to life, and *we are all witnesses* of the fact" (2:32, emphasis added).[9] The text records, not surprisingly, that "when the people heard this, they were cut to the heart and said to *Peter and the other apostles*, 'Brothers, what shall we do?'" (2:37, emphasis added). There is power and liberty in team ministry.

According to the Word, there is no such thing as the "fivefold pastor" (or, as Frank Viola calls it, *sola pastora*);[10] and a healthy appreciation for the diversity of ministry giftings brings freedom and satisfaction. It is true that all elders must function on some level as shepherds (see Acts 20:28 and 1 Peter 5:3, where the Greek verb for *shepherd/pastor* is used), for which reason I understand why the leaders of local churches are almost always referred to as *pastors*. But the obvious question is this: If *pastor* is just one of the fivefold ministry gifts listed in Ephesians 4:11 (apostle, prophet, evangelist, pastor, teacher),[11] why does it seem that almost all leaders are pastors? What has become of the other ministry giftings?

What makes this all the more striking is that the Greek noun *poimen*, "pastor/shepherd," is used with reference to a church leader *only once* in the entire New Testament—namely in Ephesians 4:11. Otherwise it always refers to Jesus.[12] In contrast with this, outside of Ephesians 4:11, *apostle* is found five times (with reference to someone other than the twelve apostles or Paul), *prophet* is found eleven times, *evangelist* is found twice, and *teacher* occurs eleven times.[13] Yet in many Pentecostal circles, if you are "in the ministry" you are a pastor, unless you travel and speak, in which case you are an evangelist. But these are the ministry callings mentioned *least* in the New Testament![14] Where have all the others gone?[15]

Perhaps, dear pastor, you are truly called to be the point man of your congregation and the senior leader of your ministry team. But could it be that your primary calling is not pastoral? Perhaps your real gifting is evangelism, and you consistently win the lost and equip the members for evangelistic action, deepening their passion for the work of the Lord. As the recognized leader you cast the vision for the flock and oversee the team. But rather than try to fill the role of "pastor"—especially in terms of our current model—perhaps the key to greater fruit bearing is to identify the truly pastoral people in your midst and empower *them* to help shepherd the flock. Is this too revolutionary a concept?

Not only will you be released (wonderfully, I might add), but the congregation will be far healthier. This also goes a long way toward dismantling the pastoral fraternity, since the importance of other ministry gifts will be realized, along with our need for one another—not just in the local assembly, but in an entire city. You will find that you are much more effective when you function in your true gifting and calling (although I stress again that all of us in leadership, to one extent or another, function as shepherds).

Paul taught that this fivefold expression was absolutely essential "to prepare God's people for works of service, so that the body of Christ may be built up until we all reach unity in the faith and in the knowledge of the Son of God and become mature, attaining to the whole measure of the fullness of Christ" (Ephesians 4:12–13; see further verses 14–15). We dare not minimize this!

4. Do away with the notion of Christian leaders-for-hire (or of ministers seeking jobs or positions), also discarding the concept of a non-elder governing board. Certainly it is right and biblical for those who preach the Gospel full time to make their living from the Gospel (see 1 Corinthians 9:7–14), and leaders are sometimes invited by churches to candidate for a "ministerial position." But the church is not a business (or company or franchise) and, ideally speaking, leaders should not be "hired" and "fired" as much as "called in" and "sent out," unless some kind of moral failure or doctrinal error leads to their removal. Yet in many cases a minister will take a position based on salary and benefits, or a church will fire a pastor based on petty congregational preferences—and none of this may have anything to do with the will of God. How different it is to think of leaders as called by God to do an eternal work rather than as hired shepherds with ministerial "staffs."

The notion of a board running the church is also unbiblical, unless the word *board* refers to the governing elders.[16] Otherwise we must reject this binding, archaic worldly system of a church board comprised of influential or long-standing (but not necessarily spiritual) members who can constrain or even cripple the leader(s). Where is there an ounce of support for this in the Word? What New Testament model does it follow? And how does it enhance the work of the ministry or advance the Kingdom?

I am aware that many boards have their hands full dealing with maverick, impetuous pastors who can destroy a church if not kept in check. Some congregations have been burned too many times by unaccountable leaders. But my appeal is to one and all alike: to the leaders, to walk in humility and mutual accountability, seeking the Lord and discerning His will in unity; to the non-elder board, to be dismantled and let the elders lead the way and carry the decision-making responsibility. For some churches this is asking a lot. But I warned you in the very first chapter of this book: *Revolution*, rightly understood, is a disturbing word, and a revolution that costs nothing is worth nothing. How revolutionary do you really want to be?

5. Lastly I appeal to all believers in the local congregations: Let your leaders know that you are with them and that you are there to serve, to get involved, to be used in ministry. Don't just sit there; do something! Be a support and encouragement; be a laborer; be a solution-finder rather than a faultfinder. And be broad-minded, welcoming positive change.

You have no idea how "sheep bit" some shepherds are, or how insecure many of them are in their work—and a big reason for this insecurity is the failure of some flocks to affirm their leaders. Empower them to be who God called them to be. Help to release them in their anointing and create an atmosphere of faith, not friction, when they minister the Word. Encourage them to spend quality time alone with the Lord. Your strength is tied in with theirs!

Already I can feel the air getting cleaner. Already I can feel burdens lifting. Already I can feel hope rising afresh. As I said at the beginning of this chapter, there *is* a better way. Are you still coming along?

# 9

# By What Authority Do You Do These Things?

### GETTING TO THE CRUX OF THE MATTER

I love him [Moody] and reverence him as I do no other man on earth. To me he has seemed for years a man full of the Holy Ghost. The only change I see in him now is a growth of conscious power and an ability for speaking with added weight and deeper conviction. He is wholly and thoroughly conscious that it is all of God. Praying alone with him, I found him humble as a child before God. Out in the work with him I found him bold as a lion before men. No hesitation, no shrinking, no timidity; speaking with authority, speaking as an ambassador of the most high God.

from the diary of Major D. W. Whittle
cited in W. R. Moody, *The Life of Dwight L. Moody*

Though never ordained, Moody preached to more people than anyone else of his time.

*Dictionary of Christianity in America*

No more fundamental religious question can be raised than, "By what authority?" It is antecedent to all other questions about living and thinking.

Bruce Shelley, *By What Authority?*

The theological meaning of authority is an enduring issue in the West due to the breakdown of obedience to traditional sources and institutions of authority during the Reformation and the Enlightenment. The division of Christians into Catholics and Protestants, and then into the various Protestant movements and churches became the occasion for intense religious and political conflict leading to persecution, revolution and war.

*Dictionary of Christianity in America*

*If you have not read chapter 6, "Revolutionary, Not 'Rebelutionary,'" don't continue reading! First study that chapter carefully, digest its contents and then continue here. If you absolutely refuse, you are showing signs of a wrong attitude!*

William Booth. John Bunyan. Martin Luther. John Owen. William Seymour. John Wesley. George Whitefield. Roger Williams. What do these men have in common?

All of them were famous Christian leaders, each in his own distinctive way. Booth founded the Salvation Army, spreading its radical and compassionate message to more than eighty nations. Bunyan wrote *The Pilgrim's*

141

*Progress,* one of the most translated, widely read books in history. Luther provided the spark that ignited the Protestant Reformation. Owen was the most learned of the Puritan theologians. Seymour was the principal leader in the Azusa Street outpouring. Wesley was the father of the Methodist movement. Whitefield was the greatest preacher of the Great Awakening. Williams paved the way for the concept of the (proper) separation of church and state. These men not only touched their own generation but left behind a legacy that continues to touch lives today.

But these men have something else in common: Each one of them went against the religious grain of his day. Each one of them was a pioneer often scorned and rejected by the Church establishment. Each one of them had a conflict with the contemporary spiritual authorities, ultimately having to obey God rather than man. Yet we hail them today as heroes.

According to Leonard Ravenhill, this is always the fate of the prophet—and of the spiritual pioneer as well:

> He is the villain of today and the hero of tomorrow.
> He is excommunicated while alive and exalted when dead.
> He is dishonored with epithets when breathing and honored with epitaphs when dead.
> He is friendless while living and famous when dead.
> He is against the establishment in ministry; then he is established as a saint by posterity.[1]

This is also the way prophetic, pioneering *movements* are treated, and if it has happened once, it has happened a thousand times—or, more realistically, tens of thousands of times. The tune may be different but the words of the song are always the same: "By what authority do

142

you do these things? Who gave you the right?" That is how the established spiritual leadership opposes the new voice or move or church or message.

Jesus Himself experienced this kind of resistance. After making His triumphal entry into Jerusalem, He entered the Temple and cleared out the moneychangers, overturning their tables and proclaiming: "It is written . . . 'My house will be called a house of prayer,' but you are making it a 'den of robbers' " (Matthew 21:13). The Messiah had come to do His Father's bidding.

The blind and lame came to Him to receive healing, and the excitement was such that even children shouted His praises in the Temple. What a glorious scene this must have been! The religious leaders, however, were indignant (Matthew 21:14–15).

The next morning He cursed a barren fig tree, and it withered on the spot (21:19). Then He returned to the Temple courts, "and, while he was teaching, the chief priests and the elders of the people came to him. 'By what authority are you doing these things?' they asked. 'And who gave you this authority?' " (21:23).

Isn't this remarkable? The blind and lame had been healed the day before, apparently right before these leaders' eyes, and that very morning a fig tree had withered at Jesus' rebuke. (The leaders may have heard about this as well.) The whole city was stirred over His coming, recognizing Him as the long-awaited Messiah. Yet the leaders had only one question: By what authority are You doing these things? Who gave You the right?

"We are the religious leaders here, and You are challenging our system and upsetting our apple cart. You drive out the moneychangers, attack our whole method of operation, work all kinds of miracles and now set up shop in our Temple, teaching Your own doctrines. What right do You have to do this? Who gave You permission?

Which group is sanctioning Your activities? What makes You think You have divine authority backing You?"

This is the standard line in an all-too-familiar story, a story that is repeated every time God gives birth to something new in the midst of His people. The new thing is generally rejected and scorned before it is accepted and embraced. As Paul explained to the Galatians, "Now you, brothers, like Isaac, are children of promise. At that time the son born in the ordinary way [literally, according to the flesh] persecuted the son born by the power of the Spirit. It is the same now" (Galatians 4:28–29)— and *now, today,* once more.

Even if something was originally born in the power of the Spirit, once it loses its fire, its vigor, its freshness— in other words, once it becomes ordinary or traditional or natural—it will persecute the new thing born in the power of the Spirit. That which *used to be* a new wineskin will reject that which *is* a new wineskin. Or, to express it another way, once a movement becomes the establishment, its very nature, fixed and established, causes it to reject any fresh, new, spiritual movement. The establishment dislikes change. It has become too comfortable.

And when you buck the system, even if God Himself has raised you up for this very purpose, you can expect to hear the same refrain: "By what authority are you doing this?" This is the voice of traditional religion at its worst. God's words and deeds are not important. Tradition is!

In Acts 4, after the healing of the man lame from birth (recorded in Acts 3), the religious leaders called Peter and the apostles to account for this outstanding miracle, asking them, "By what power or what name did you do this?" (Acts 4:7). That is to say, "We don't care that an incredible work of God just took place. We don't care that the Lord has graciously extended His healing hand. We only care about one thing: Who gave you the power to do this? In what name [a "name" was something closely associated with authority in the ancient world] did you accomplish this feat?" How blind this attitude is!

> "What are we going to do with these men?" [the religious leaders] asked. "Everybody living in Jerusalem knows they have done an outstanding miracle, and we cannot deny it. But to stop this thing from spreading any further among the people, we must warn these men to speak no longer to anyone in this name." Then they called them in again and commanded them not to speak or teach at all in the name of Jesus.
>
> Acts 4:16–18

They could not deny the miracle, but because it did not originate under their auspices, did not have their approval and, worst of all, conflicted with their authority, they tried to shut it down. This is the religious way. It stands against spiritual progress and, when it resists the Word of God, must itself be resisted.

Consider the origin of the Protestant Reformation: By what authority did Martin Luther defy the Church of his day? We commend him as a courageous hero for taking his bold stand before the Diet of Worms on April 18, 1521, sealed by his famous words: "My conscience is captive to the Word of God. . . . Here I stand, I can do no other. God help me. Amen!"

The authorities of his day, backed by hundreds of years of sacred traditions, united against him. What gave him the right to go against the grain? What made him right and them wrong? What gave him the right to face down his leaders and hold fast to his doctrine of justification by faith? According to Luther's colleague Philip Melanchthon, this doctrine—the norm for the New Testament Church but a novelty for the Church of Luther's day—was "delivered to us by divine authority."[2] In other words, it was delivered by a nonnegotiable rule that stands higher than all earthly authority, the final arbiter in all matters of faith and conscience—the Scriptures. There is no higher authority than the authority of God.[3]

When the Word goes against our Church traditions or personal preferences, we must obey the Word. When the Word goes against an angelic revelation or prophetic message, we must obey the Word (see Galatians 1:8–12). Luther had no choice but to follow the plain sense of Scripture, even if the Church of his day opposed him.[4]

"But," you ask, "wasn't the Church of Luther's day almost completely apostate? He had no choice but to go outside the organized Church to obey the Word of God."

That is a good point, but it is not as simple as it sounds. Luther never intended to go outside the Church of his day when he first posted his 95 Theses in Wittenberg. He simply wanted to stimulate discussion among the theologians, not realizing at the outset that a split would become inevitable. Luther himself did not initially grasp just how apostate the Church of his day had become and how his own scriptural views could not possibly fit within the existing spiritual system.[5]

This is often the pattern with new movements within the Body. The dissenting leaders simply want to stimulate discussion and bring about change within the existing structure. They do not want to reject the existing structure; they want to reform or restore it. They do not intend to start a new church or movement or denomination or organization, often being deeply devoted to their home church or movement or denomination. They end up giving birth to something new only when: (1) they are put out of the existing structure and told they are no longer welcome there; or (2) they realize that their presence in the existing structure is disruptive and that they are no longer received there; or (3) they find that they are being restricted in their calling and are no longer able to go against their convictions; or (4) they sense a clear leading from the Lord to move on to something new.

Sometimes the break with the existing structure is gradual and subtle, emerging over a period of years. At other times the break is sudden and jarring, accompanied by strong accusations from both sides.[6]

Consider the origin of the Methodists. By what authority did John Wesley preach throughout England, Scotland, Ireland and Wales, setting up small groups of disciples (called class meetings) in every city where he won converts? Look at what he faced:

> Outside [of a few areas] there was terrific opposition. Most of the clergy thought Wesley out of his wits and refused him their pulpits. Bishop Butler (of [the widely respected Christian work] the *Analogy*), hauling Wesley before him, and saying coldly that the accounts of the conversions he heard, and which Wesley joyfully confirmed, were "very extraordinary indeed," asked him by what authority he preached in his diocese. The general authority of ordination that Wesley claimed was not enough for Butler, who forbade him to continue. That did not stop Wesley, but the Bishop took no action. Samuel Wesley grew ever more aghast at his brothers [John and Charles], and implored them to return to sanity. When he heard of John's interview with Butler, he warned them lest they should, not be excommunicated from the Church (he deplored the feebleness of its discipline), but themselves excommunicate the Church, a prophecy which fell on deaf ears, and which, since he died in November 1739, he did not live to see justified. Old Mrs. Wesley was at first averse to this new faith; then, one day, at Holy Communion, she felt that at last all her sins were really forgiven her,

147

and her criticism ceased. Lay opposition was more furious still.[7]

The religious leadership of the Church of England opposed Wesley; many common people (termed here "lay opposition") opposed him; even his own family opposed him. Yet none of this stopped him. Wesley was convinced by the Word, by the Spirit, and by his own experience that the Gospel he preached was true. And although he was never formally excommunicated, therefore, in a sense he did what his brother Samuel feared he would do: By his teachings and his new "Methodist" movement, he excommunicated the Church of England, although he remained loyal to it for life and never renounced his ties. The Methodist separation happened gradually, without a definite break.

Sadly, one century later, when William Booth started the Salvation Army, ministering to the poorest of the poor in East London, many Methodists persecuted and opposed him. By what authority did he begin his new work? Who gave him the right? At first he was vilified and reviled. But when he died, all of London mourned for him. City offices closed, and during "Booth's lying-in-state, 150,000 people filed by the casket, and 40,000 people, including Queen Mary, attended his funeral."[8]

What about the Baptists? B. L. Shelley, writing in the *Dictionary of Christianity in America,* had this to say about their origins:

> Baptists, at first a handful of radicals on the fringe of the Puritan movement, agreed with the Puritan majority in their criticism of the Anglican Church, but they disagreed with most Puritans at two important points: (1) they said that church membership should be limited, not only to those families who could testify of the grace of God, but that even children of believers must be

148

*Baptists*

denied baptism and church membership until they too can personally confess their faith in Christ; (2) they argued that God had instituted the state as well as the church, and that the two were designed by God to serve two distinct purposes. While the state was intended to bear the sword of justice, the church was designed to worship, preach and grow by voluntary means alone, freed of the state's power.[9]

Think of it! The Baptists at first were "a handful of radicals on the fringe of the Puritan movement," yet today they number well over thirty million in the United States alone. By what authority did they break from their Puritan brethren and begin their own distinctive work? Who gave them the right? And how do the various Baptist denominations today view groups within their ranks that cannot accept their particular doctrinal slant and feel compelled to break away? Are they sometimes recognized as trailblazers or are they generally labeled as troublemakers? By what scriptural criteria is the establishment always right in its own eyes while those protesting against the establishment are always wrong?

Consider the life of Roger Williams (1603–1683), the founder of Rhode Island and regarded by many Baptists as one of their great spiritual fathers. He planted America's very first Baptist church in 1639, and according to the *Dictionary of Christianity in America*, "Williams's original influence was greatest among his near co-religionists, the Baptists. It was through the Baptists that Williams's thought and reputation was transmitted to the young nation for whom Williams became a folk hero in the nineteenth century."[10]

But Williams was a breakaway religious leader himself. After becoming a Puritan, apparently while studying at Cambridge, he had a change of views sailing en route to America:

> On board ship, Williams, after an intensive study of the New Testament, concluded that in order to be truly biblical, the Puritans in New England should explicitly separate from the Church of England. There followed a succession of clashes with the Massachusetts authorities as Williams criticized the Puritan establishment for a variety of practices, especially for expropriating Native American land without negotiations and for having the civil magistrates attempt to enforce the first four of the Ten Commandments. On October 9, 1635, the colonial General Court (legislature) banished him to England, but before he could be deported, he fled with his family and a few companions to the uninhabited regions to the south, outside the limits of Massachusetts, and in the summer of 1636 founded there a settlement which he named Providence.[11]

So Providence, and with it the colony of Rhode Island, was founded by a man fleeing deportation to England by order of the General Court due to his religious nonconformity! It was in Providence that Williams made his mark:

> As leader of the new colony, Williams purchased land from the Narragansett Indians and distributed it for use, befriended the Native Americans and learned their language, and during the Pequot War (1637) served all New England as a negotiator to restore peace to the region. In Providence he adopted the principle that "God requireth not an uniformity of Religion" and saw to it that all individuals and religious bodies enjoyed what he called "soul liberty," that is, religious freedom. . . .

And how did this teaching that "God requireth not an uniformity of Religion" (meaning that God does not require everyone to conform to the same religious norm) with its emphasis on "soul liberty" affect Williams personally?

> For the remainder of his life Williams would be a religious loner searching for a church which he could recognize as created in the image of the first apostles. In the end, he clung tenaciously to his basic Calvinist theology and to his belief in religious liberty and separation of church and state, and died an independent evangelical Christian without a denomination.[12]

Today every American is indebted to this "religious loner" who "died an independent evangelical Christian without a denomination." As Church historian R. D. Linder noted,

> In many ways, Williams's Rhode Island, with its stress on freedom, individualism and being a place "where no man should be molested for his conscience"—and not Puritan New England with its emphasis on order, community and the mission of a "city on a hill"—was the prototype of the future American republic.[13]

Yet Williams "could never have known that his views concerning the separation of church and state would become one of the enduring facets of American experience."[14] The question remains: By what authority did Roger Williams stand his ground? Who gave him the right?

Consider the origins of the modern Pentecostal movement. Its roots are generally traced to Charles Parham's Bible school in Topeka, Kansas, where students received the baptism of the Holy Spirit with the evidence of speaking in tongues beginning January 1, 1901. But the great explosion came at Azusa Street in 1906 under the leadership of William J. Seymour, and from there the power of Pentecost spread around the globe. Today there are approximately five hundred million Pentecostal/ charismatic believers worldwide, making up the largest single part of the Protestant church.

How did Seymour end up at Azusa Street? He had relocated from Houston to Los Angeles in January 1906 at the invitation of a Holiness church there, but when he started preaching on tongues as the initial evidence of the baptism of the Spirit, he was barred from the church—literally. They actually locked him out of the mission. So he began to hold meetings at a house on Bonnie Brae Street until the porch collapsed because of all the people. It was only then that they found the abandoned building at Azusa Street—a small building that seated about three hundred—and started holding meetings there.

By what authority did Seymour do this? Under whose covering? Who gave him the right? Could it be that God sent him? Could it be that God raised up the work and backed the work?

Let's take this one step further. Consider the origins of the Assemblies of God, the world's largest Pentecostal denomination, as noted on its website.[15] How was the Assemblies formed? According to its Internet statement, as the Pentecostal fire spread from Azusa Street,

> Reports of what was taking place were carried in scores of periodicals and other publications that sprang up with the movement. Spontaneous revivals also began to break out about that time in other parts of the world and on various mission fields.
>
> The Pentecostal aspects of the revival were not generally welcomed by the established churches and participants in the movement soon found themselves outside existing religious bodies. They were forced to seek

152

their own places of worship, and soon there were hundreds of distinctly Pentecostal congregations.

By 1914, many ministers and laymen alike had begun to realize the rapid spread of the revival, and the many evangelistic outreaches it spawned had created a number of practical problems. The need arose for formal recognition of ministers as well as approval and support of missionaries, with full accounting of funds. In addition, there was a growing demand for doctrinal unity, gospel literature, and a permanent Bible training school.

These concerned leaders realized that to protect and preserve the results of the revival the thousands of newly Spirit-baptized believers should be united in a cooperative fellowship. In 1914 about 300 preachers and laymen gathered from 20 states and several foreign countries for a "general council" in Hot Springs, Arkansas, to discuss and take action on the growing need.

The five reasons they listed for calling the meeting were: doctrinal unity, conservation of the work, foreign missions interests, chartering churches under a common name for legal purposes, and the need for a Bible training school.[16]

By what authority did these three hundred preachers and "laymen" do this? Which governing body approved this? Who gave them the right to birth this new movement? They would say that they had no choice. They could do no other. They were only moving with the Spirit and obeying God. It was inevitable!

And notice carefully these words: "The Pentecostal aspects of the revival were not generally welcomed by the established churches and participants in the movement soon found themselves outside existing religious bodies. They were forced to seek their own places of worship, and soon there were hundreds of distinctly Pentecostal congregations."

How enlightening! It was "the established churches" that rejected the new movement (as always), and "participants in the movement soon found themselves outside existing religious bodies"—meaning they were either put out of these bodies or left voluntarily. Were there no churches in which these Pentecostals could feel at home? Were there no religious bodies that were not "established"?

The official statement just cited provides the answer: *They were forced* to seek their own places of worship, and soon there were hundreds of distinctly Pentecostal congregations" (emphasis added). Assemblies historian Edith Blumhofer states things even more strongly: These founders "nurtured an intense dislike for established denominations."[17] And so once again history repeated itself.

What happens today if a new move of the Spirit comes to those within the denomination, and the participants in that move feel that their own churches have become established? What happens if they, too, find themselves "outside existing religious bodies," just as their spiritual forefathers did? What happens if they, too, feel "forced to seek their own places of worship, and soon there [are] hundreds of [new] congregations" with a fresh Pentecostal distinctive? Will these believers be blessed by their former leaders and encouraged to go for it, or will they be branded as independent and ungrateful?

Why were the founders of the Puritans or Methodists or Baptists or Assemblies of God right in breaking away and forming their own movement in their day, but it is wrong for someone to break away from them and form a new work today? Why is a movement accepted only once it becomes "established"—by which time a new movement needs to be birthed because the wineskins have become old? The original movement began because it rejected the established churches of its day!

154

Consider the ministries of some of the giants in Church history. We think of John Bunyan as a humble, beloved man of God. But not everyone loved him. He spent years in prison for refusing to comply with the restrictions and mandates of the leading church of his day:

> In 1660 old acts against Nonconformists were revived. Meeting houses were closed; all persons were required under severe penalties to attend their parish church; it became illegal to conduct worship services except in accordance with Anglican ritual. Bunyan continued to preach in barns, in private homes, under the trees, or in a church if an invitation came. He was arrested in November 1660 on his way to conduct a religious service about twelve miles from Bedford. In 1661 his wife Elizabeth made a moving plea for him before the judge in Bedford. . . . After 1668 he began to have times of parole, although his formal pardon did not come until 1672.[18]

So the organized Church banned John Bunyan, the best-selling Christian author of all time, and forced him "to preach in barns, in private homes, under the trees, or in a church if an invitation came." Then he was imprisoned for preaching in these places. And it was from prison that Bunyan wrote most of his classic works.

*Christian History* magazine notes that "when local magistrates sentenced Bunyan to imprisonment unless he promised them he would not preach, *he refused,* declaring that he would remain in prison till the moss grew on his eyelids rather than fail to do what God had commanded him to do." In fact, "Bunyan would have been released from prison if he would agree not to preach in 'unlawful' or unlicensed assemblies. His own writings attest that he was given every opportunity to

155

'conform.' It was a compromise he would not make."[19] Compromise was simply not in his vocabulary.

Why, then, was it right for him to refuse to bow to the unbiblical practices of the Church of his day, following his conscience and the Word of God, while it is wrong for someone to do the same today? Why do we consider him righteous for the stand he took while the authorities of his day called him rebellious?

Consider the ministry of George Whitefield (1714–1770), a man described by some Church historians as the greatest preacher of any era. By what authority did he begin to preach in the open fields? To do so was outlandish, and no one had ever heard of such a preposterous, almost heretical idea. Yet we hail him today as the pioneer of mass evangelism! He is recognized as an innovative, self-sacrificing evangelist who preached himself into the grave, speaking to crowds of up to thirty thousand people without amplification. Who gave him the right to do this? Certainly not the Church leaders of his day.[20]

Or consider the towering figure of John Owen, the chaplain of Oliver Cromwell. While Owen was studying at Oxford, William Laud became chancellor and instituted "Romish innovations" in the school—innovations that Owen believed were unbiblical and therefore to be resisted, even though "the penalty of resistance [was] nothing less than expulsion from the university."[21]

Yet this was an easy choice for Owen, since his mind was "delivered by the fear of God from every other fear." After all, this was his spiritual heritage. The Puritans were used to paying for their views with their own blood and bodies, sometimes burned, sometimes butchered.

One of his biographers believes that these words of Owen, written many years later, explain why he stood his ground at Oxford:

They [believers] will receive nothing, practice nothing, own nothing in his worship, but what is of his appointment. They know that from the foundation of the world he never did allow, nor ever will, that in any thing the will of the creatures should be the measure of his honor, or the principle of his worship, either as to matter or manner. . . .

Owen claimed it was the concept, therefore,

that the church has power to institute and appoint any thing or ceremony belonging to the worship of God, either as to matter or to manner, beyond the orderly observance of such circumstances as necessarily attend such ordinances as Christ himself has instituted, [that] lies at the bottom of all the horrible superstition and idolatry, of all the confusion, blood, persecution, and wars, that have for so long a season spread themselves over the face of the Christian world; and that it is the design of a great part of the Book of the Revelation to make a discovery of this truth.

What a statement! It is the Church's instituting and appointing of things beyond what Jesus Himself instituted that "lies at the bottom of all the horrible superstition and idolatry, of all the confusion, blood, persecution, and wars, that have for so long a season spread themselves over the face of the Christian world." Owen claimed that this was God's primary issue with England.

And I doubt not but that the great controversy which God has had with this nation for so many years, and which he has pursued with so much anger and indignation, was upon this account, that, contrary to the glorious light of the Gospel, which shone among us, the wills and fancies of men, under the name of order, decency, and authority of the church (a chimera that none knew what it was, nor wherein the power did con-

157

sist, nor in whom reside), were imposed on men in the ways and worship of God. . . .

And what happened when the Church claimed authority beyond the authority of the Lord? Owen minced no words:

> To [the end] that Jesus Christ might be deposed from the sole power of lawmaking in his church,—that the true husband might be thrust aside, and adulterers of his spouse embraced,—that taskmasters might be appointed in and over his house, which he never gave to his church, Ephesians 4:11,—that a ceremonious, pompous, outward show-worship, drawn from Pagan, Judaical, and Antichristian observances, might be introduced; of all which there is not one word, little, or iota in the whole book of God. This, then, they who hold communion with Christ are careful of,—they will admit nothing, practice nothing, in the worship of God, private or public, but what they have his warrant for. Unless it comes in his name, with 'Thus saith the Lord Jesus,' they will not hear an angel from heaven.[22]

This, then, is the crux of the matter, spoken so clearly by John Owen himself: Human beings, especially Church leaders appointed by the Head of the Church Himself, have no right whatsoever to depose the Lord Jesus "from the sole power of lawmaking in his church,—that the true husband might be thrust aside, and adulterers of his spouse embraced,—that taskmasters might be appointed in and over his house, which he never gave to his church." And all this comes from "the wills and fancies of men, under the name of order, decency, and authority of the church." We cannot bow down to this!

Rather, Owen allows for one ultimate allegiance for every believer: "They will admit nothing, practice nothing, in the worship of God, private or public, but what they have his warrant for. Unless it comes in his name, with 'Thus saith the Lord Jesus,' they will not hear an angel from heaven." Jesus has the final word, and it is to that authoritative word we must bow. Dare we rebel against the Lord?

# 10

# Have You Read the Epistle of Jacob Lately?

## RESTORING OUR JEWISH ROOTS

Well, now, I don't know in detail where they got it from, but I can guess approximately. Here at Wittenberg, in our parish church, there is a sow carved into the stone under which lie young pigs and Jews who are sucking; behind the sow stands a rabbi who is lifting up the right leg of the sow, raises the behind of the sow, bows down and looks with great effort into the Talmud [the most sacred books of traditional Judaism] under the sow, as if he wanted to read and see something most difficult and exceptional. . . . For among the Germans it is said of someone who pretends to great wisdom without good cause: "Where did he read that? On the behind of the sow [crudely expressed]."

Martin Luther, *Vom Schem Hamphoras*
(Concerning the Unutterable Name of the Lord)

You, you Jews. I say, do I address you; you, who till this very day, deny the Son of God. How long, poor wretches, will ye not believe the truth? Truly I doubt whether a Jew can be really human. . . . I lead out from its den a monstrous animal, and show it as a laughing stock in the amphitheatre of the world, in the sight of all the people. I bring thee forward, thou Jew, thou brute beast, in the sight of all men.

> Peter the Venerable, twelfth century
> Known as "the meekest of men,
> a model of Christian charity"

If some of the branches have been broken off, and you, though a wild olive shoot, have been grafted in among the others and now share in the nourishing sap from the olive root, do not boast over those branches. If you do, consider this: You do not support the root, but the root supports you.

> Paul the apostle, Romans 11:17–18

I want to introduce you to a dynamic, eloquent minister of the Gospel who is making a great impact for the Lord around the world, a man known for his godliness, sacrifice and compassion, a man whose only blemish is his recent series of sermons titled "Kill the Niggers!" Would you like to meet him?

"You've got to be kidding!" you might say. "There's no way godliness and racism can mix, no way love for God and hatred for man can be found in the same spiritual package."

I agree. In fact, I must confess I made the whole thing up. But what you are about to read is *not* made up, although I am quite sure you will wish it were. So be forewarned: The following information may be dangerous to your spiritual tranquility. You are about to see some of the most widely respected leaders in Church history in what for you may be a new and disturbing light.

The first leader, a powerful preacher who lived in the city of Antioch more than fifteen hundred years ago, was known for his Christlike character and moving messages. His name was John, but after his death people called him Chrysostom (Golden-Mouthed) because of his eloquent speech. He was later canonized as a saint.

Although history hails Chrysostom as a mighty man of God, one widely revered (especially in Greek Orthodox circles) until this day, he delivered a series of seven sermons against the Jews—sermons famous for their venom and for helping fuel the fires of anti-Semitism through the centuries. Sermons famous for lines such as these:

> I know that many people hold a high regard for the Jew, and consider their way of life worthy of respect at the present time. This is why I am hurrying to pull up this fatal notion by the roots. . . .

> The synagogue is worse than a brothel. . . . It is the den of scoundrels and the repair of wild beasts . . . the temple of demons devoted to idolatrous cults . . . the refuge of brigands and debauchees, and the cavern of devils. [It is] a criminal assembly of Jews . . . a place of meeting for the assassins of Christ . . . a house worse than a drinking shop . . . a den of thieves; a house of ill fame, a dwelling of iniquity, the refuge of devils, a gulf and abyss of perdition. . . . I would say the same things about their souls.

> When animals have been fattened by having all they want to eat, they get stubborn and hard to manage. . . . When animals are unfit for work, they are marked for slaughter, and this is the very thing which the Jews have experienced. By making themselves unfit for work, they

have become ready for slaughter. This is why Christ said, "As for my enemies, who did not want me to reign over them, bring them here and slay them before me."[1]

As for me, I hate the synagogue. . . . I hate the Jews for the same reason.[2]

Is it any wonder that "not long after these sermons were preached, there were several violent outbursts against Jews in Antioch, with its great synagogue demolished"?[3] As Catholic author Malcolm Hay sadly observed: "For many centuries the Jews listened to the echo of those three words of St. John Chrysostom, the Golden-Mouthed: 'God hates you.'"[4] Yes, God hates the Jews! Such sentiments are found throughout fifteen hundred years' worth of "Christian literature"—and they are hardly hidden or obscure.

How tragic and shameful it is that Bible colleges and seminaries teach exhaustive courses on Church history, focusing on "Church Fathers" such as Chrysostom but failing to mention his anti-Semitism. This is inexcusable. As Edward Flannery, a prominent Catholic historian, once commented,

> The vast majority of Christians, even well educated, are all but totally ignorant of what happened to Jews in history and of the culpable involvement of the Church. . . . It is little exaggeration to state that those pages of history Jews have committed to memory are the very ones that have been torn from Christian (and secular) history books.[5]

"But," you say, "Chrysostom is not exactly a household name. And he lived such a long time ago. I doubt that more recent, better-known Christian leaders spewed such hateful trash."

I wish you were right. Instead, the opposite is true. Let's go back to Germany, not fifteen hundred years ago, but five hundred years ago. And instead of Chrysostom, a man not as widely known today, let's look at one of the greatest heroes of the faith, a man who singlehandedly took on the corrupt Church of his day and brought us back to the Word of God, the man who launched the Protestant Reformation—and a man some have referred to as "the John the Baptist of Adolf Hitler."[6] Let me introduce you afresh to Martin Luther.

Yes, Martin Luther—the Luther who was considered a genius by Nazi leaders, whose counsel Hitler followed to the letter in his first violent anti-Semitic acts, whose writings against the Jews are so vulgar that translators cannot render them into English without using profanity.[7]

"But," you say, "didn't you make reference to Luther earlier in this book—even in the last chapter—commending him for his righteous stands?" Yes, I did, for two reasons: First, the good things he did are undeniable, and we are all indebted to him for his courage and faith. Without him we would not be where we are today. That can never be taken away. Second, this makes the contrast with his vulgar anti-Semitism all the more striking.

The tragic fact is that even though some of Luther's colleagues rejected his anti-Semitic writings, his views were hardly exceptional in his day. Extreme, perhaps, but still reflecting the norm. In the words of Erasmus, Luther's contemporary and theological opponent, referring to the Jews, "Who is there among us who does not hate this race of men? If it is Christian to hate the Jews, here we are all Christians in profusion."[8]

In 1961 Holocaust historian Raul Hilberg published his landmark study *The Destruction of the European Jews*,[9] containing the now-famous charts demonstrating that all the anti-Semitic policies set in place by the Nazis, with the sole exception of extermination, had already been instituted by "the Church" in previous centuries. It was "the Church" that first passed discriminatory laws against the Jews, forcing them to wear a yellow star, herding them into ghettos and even expelling them from their countries. (Hilberg provides far more details than this.) The Nazis merely renewed previously instituted anti-Semitic measures—but with a vengeance and cruelty and systematic hatred never before imagined.

On the flip side, history records uniquely "Christian" atrocities committed by "the Church" that even the Nazis did not commit—like herding the Jews of a city into a synagogue and burning it to the ground while marching around it and singing "Christ, We Adore Thee." The Crusaders did this in Jerusalem in July 1099 after overcoming the city's Muslim and Jewish resistance. Ironically the Crusader uniforms were emblazoned with crosses, something not forgotten by Jews through the centuries whose ancestors were burned alive by these "Christians." This also explains why many Jewish believers today do not refer to their evangelistic outreaches as "crusades."[10]

Returning to Martin Luther, early in his ministry he had high hopes that the Jewish people would embrace Jesus as Messiah *en masse*. Luther actually wrote a small booklet in 1523 titled "That Jesus Christ Was Born a Jew," in which he spoke scornfully about the terrible way the Church had treated the Jews until that time. He wrote: "If the Apostles, who were also Jews, had dealt with us Gentiles as we Gentiles deal with the Jews there would never have been a Christian among the Gentiles. . . . We in our turn ought to treat the Jews in a brotherly manner in order that we might convert some of them. . . . We are but Gentiles, while the Jews are of the line-

165

age of Christ. We are aliens and in-laws; they are blood relatives, cousins and brothers of our Lord."

But there were no mass conversions of the Jews, and Luther, old, sick and outraged with Jewish polemics against Jesus, wrote a series of horrific anti-Semitic publications, culminating in his infamous writings of 1543. He stated that "it is not my opinion that I can write against the Jews in the hope of converting them," since "to convert the Jews . . . is about as possible as converting the Devil."

He explained:

> A Jew or a Jewish heart is as hard as stone and iron and cannot be moved by any means. . . . In sum, they are the devil's children damned to hell. . . . We cannot even convert the majority of Christians and have to be satisfied with a small number; it is therefore even less possible to convert these children of the devil! Although there are many who derive the crazy notion from the 11th chapter of the Epistle to the Romans that all Jews must be converted, this is not so. St. Paul meant something quite different.[11]

For Luther the Jews were the worst enemy of all, "devils and nothing more":

> Verily, a hopeless, wicked, venomous and devilish thing is the existence of these Jews, who for fourteen hundred years have been, and still are, our pest, torment and misfortune. They are just devils and nothing more.

> Know, Christian, that next to the devil thou hast no enemy more cruel, more venomous and violent than a true Jew.[12]

What then was his counsel to the local German princes for dealing with the Jews?

First, their synagogues or churches should be set on fire, and whatever does not burn up should be covered or spread over with dirt so that no one may ever be able to see a cinder or stone of it. And this ought to be done for the honor of God and of Christianity. . . .

Secondly, their homes should likewise be broken down and destroyed. For they perpetrate the same things there that they do in their synagogues. For this reason they ought to be put under one roof or in a stable, like gypsies. . . .

Thirdly, they should be deprived of their prayerbooks and Talmuds in which such idolatry, lies, cursing and blasphemy are taught.

Fourthly, their rabbis must be forbidden under threat of death to teach any more. . . .

Fifthly, passport and traveling privileges should be absolutely forbidden to the Jews. . . .

Sixthly, they ought to be stopped from usury. All their cash and valuables of silver and gold ought to be taken from them and put aside for safekeeping.

Seventhly, let the young Jews and Jewesses be given the flail, the ax, the hoe, the spade, the distaff and spindle, and let them earn their bread by the sweat of their noses. . . .

In brief, dear princes and lords, those of you who have Jews under your rule—if my counsel does not please you, find better advice, so that you and we all can be rid of the unbearable, devilish burden of the Jews, lest we become guilty sharers before God in the lies, blasphemy, the defamation, and the curses which the mad Jews indulge in so freely and wantonly against the person of our Lord Jesus Christ, his dear mother, all Christians, all authority, and ourselves. Do not grant them protection, safe-conduct, or communion with us.... With this faithful counsel and warning I wish to cleanse and exonerate my conscience.[13]

If reading this was not terrifying enough, consider another fact: Many historians believe the Holocaust officially began on what is known as "Kristallnacht," the Night of Broken Glass, November 9–10, 1938. During this ominous two-day period, Nazi soldiers followed Luther's counsel to a tee, setting the synagogues on fire and smashing the windows of Jewish places of business, among other humiliating and even murderous acts. I had no good answer for the rabbi who first pointed out to me that the Nazis carried this out in honor of the anniversary of Luther's birth. (He was born November 10, 1483.)

In his important recent study, *Hitler's Willing Executioners*, Daniel Jonah Goldhagen points out that

> One leading Protestant churchman, Bishop Martin Sasse, published a compendium of Martin Luther's anti-semitic vitriol shortly after *Kristallnacht's* orgy of anti-Jewish violence. In the foreword to the volume, he applauded the burning of the synagogues and the coincidence of the day: "On November 10, 1938, on Luther's birthday, the synagogues are burning in Germany." The German people, he urged, ought to heed these words "of the greatest antisemite of his time, the warner of his people against the Jews."[14]

Not surprisingly Julius Streicher, one of Hitler's top henchmen and publisher of the anti-Semitic *Der Sturmer*, was asked during the Nuremberg trials for war criminals if any other publications in Germany treated the

Jewish question in an anti-Semitic way. Streicher put it well:

> Dr. Martin Luther would very probably sit in my place in the defendants' dock today, if this book had been taken into consideration by the Prosecution. In the book "The Jews and Their Lies," Dr. Martin Luther writes that the Jews are a serpent's brood and one should burn down their synagogues and destroy them. . . .[15]

So, according to Streicher, the Nazis only did what Luther urged them to do!

"But now when I read about Luther, or hear his name mentioned, I'll have mixed feelings!" you say. Well, friend, now you know how countless Jewish believers feel when they read much of Church history and hear the names of many famous Christian leaders. We have mixed feelings, too.

Now, do you really think my shock tactics at the beginning of this chapter were exaggerated? My personal library contains numerous lengthy volumes devoted to the subject of "Christian" anti-Semitism—and they make for some very painful reading.[16] In light of this, it is hardly surprising that in religious Jewish circles, Christianity became synonymous with Jew hatred, especially when you realize that other hateful, bigoted quotes from the lips of "Christian" leaders can be found in virtually every century for the last fifteen hundred years.[17]

How can this be? How could a faith founded on sacrificial love turn into such a monstrous exhibition of bigotry and hate? The answer is simple: The Church lost sight of its Jewish roots, and, just as Paul warned, ignorance turned into arrogance:

> If some of the branches have been broken off, and you, though a wild olive shoot, have been grafted in among

169

the others and now share in the nourishing sap from the olive root, do not boast over those branches. If you do, consider this: You do not support the root, but the root supports you.

Romans 11:17–18

Paul's meaning is clear. In former times, the Gentiles "were separate from Christ, excluded from citizenship in Israel and foreigners to the covenants of the promise, without hope and without God in the world. But now in Christ Jesus," he writes, "you who once were far away have been brought near through the blood of Christ" (Ephesians 2:12–13). Consequently these Gentiles are "no longer foreigners and aliens, but fellow citizens with God's people and members of God's household" (verse 19). That is gloriously true.

But this ingrafting of the nations into Israel's tree ("the commonwealth of Israel") resulted from the Jewish branches being broken off, and Paul was concerned that a wrong attitude could develop:

You will say then, "Branches were broken off so that I could be grafted in." Granted. But they were broken off because of unbelief, and you stand by faith. *Do not be arrogant, but be afraid.* For if God did not spare the natural branches, he will not spare you either. Consider therefore the kindness and sternness of God: sternness to those who fell, but kindness to you, provided that you continue in his kindness. Otherwise, you also will be cut off. And if they do not persist in unbelief, they will be grafted in, for God is able to graft them in again.

Romans 11:19–23, emphasis added

As Paul stressed throughout Romans 10–11, God is not finished with Israel! There remains a bright future for the covenant people:

170

After all, if you were cut out of an olive tree that is wild by nature, and contrary to nature were grafted into a cultivated olive tree, how much more readily will these, the natural branches, be grafted into their own olive tree! *I do not want you to be ignorant of this mystery, brothers, so that you may not be conceited:* Israel has experienced a hardening in part until the full number of the Gentiles has come in. And so all Israel will be saved. . . .

verses 24–26, emphasis added

This is the process that led to a flood of anti-Semitic sentiment and anti-scriptural teaching: As the Church became primarily Gentile (a wonderful thing in terms of the harvest of the nations), it grew ignorant of God's dealings with the Jewish people, somehow believing He was through with Israel and that their hardening was complete and permanent. This ignorance led to arrogant beliefs: "God is finished with Israel! We are the new Israel! The Church has replaced Israel!"[18]

But Paul's warning is clear: Just as God cut off the Jewish branches because of their unbelief, He could cut off—and did cut off!—the Gentile branches because of their unbelief. *Whole sections of Church history reflect the story of a Church largely cut off*—in many ways because it cut off its Jewish roots.[19]

We need a revolution here, too! If the foundations of the building have been displaced, how stable can the building be? The stark reality is that by cutting off its Jewish roots, the Church cut off a source of life as well as truth, affecting the way we think—and what we believe—as Christians.

Let me illustrate this for you with a simple name game. When I say the name *Mao Ze-dong,* what comes to mind? Probably words like *Chinese, Communist, dictator, mass murderer.* When I say the name *Albert Einstein,* what comes to mind? Probably words like *genius,*

171

*physicist, Jewish, nuclear science.* This indicates that names carry associations and conjure up images and ideas. It also indicates that certain names go together. Switching the above names to *Mao Einstein* and *Albert Ze-dong* makes for complete nonsense. The two do not match, nor do they have anything in common.

Now let's play this game with Bible names. What comes to mind when you hear the name *Miriam?* Do you think *Christian* or *Jewish? Jewish,* no doubt. How about *Mary?* You would probably say *Christian.* What if we put some names together in a strange-sounding combination, like *Mary Schwartz?* It doesn't fit, does it? How about *Miriam Schwartz?* That's better. Why? Because both *Miriam* and *Schwartz* are Jewish names, and the two names fit together. But *Mary* is hardly a Jewish name, right?

Before I answer that question, let's take this a step further. What comes to mind when you hear someone talk about Mary, the mother of Jesus? You think *Christianity.* You may even think of the Christmas story or a beautiful sculpture like Michelangelo's *Pietà.* You certainly do not think, *That's Jewish!* But if I say, "Moses, Elijah, Isaiah, Jeremiah," you think *Jewish* rather than *Christian.*

So there is a dichotomy in our thinking between the faith of the Old Testament and the faith of the New Testament, between Israel and the Church. Rather than seeing Jesus as the One who came to fulfill the faith of Moses and the prophets, we see Him primarily as the founder of a new religion called Christianity. Yet that is *not* a biblical concept. And as far as these names are concerned, *Mary* is simply the Greek-Latin form of *Miriam, Jesus* is the Greek-Latin form of *Yeshua* and *Christ* is the Greek-Latin way of saying *Messiah,* "Anointed One."

There is more. What comes to mind when you think about the names *Saul* and *Paul?* This one is simple, right? *Saul* (in the New Testament) was a Jewish leader who persecuted the Christians, then he got converted and became *Paul*, a Christian leader, correct? Not at all! Saul was a Jewish leader who *from birth* also had the name *Paul*. (One was a Hebrew name, the other a Greek name.)[20] At one point in his life he persecuted fellow Jews who believed that Yeshua was the Jewish Messiah, and this was well before they were first called "Christians." Then he repented of his sins and embraced Yeshua as Messiah. End of story.

He never persecuted members of a different religion, nor did he convert to another religion. He did not take on a new name after his supposed conversion, nor, as some teach, did he temporarily backslide into Judaism by taking a vow or going to the Temple in Jerusalem (see Acts 18:18; 21:17–27). He was a Jew until his dying day—and a faithful Jew at that (see Acts 23:1, 6; 26:1–8).

Now, as revolutionary as some of this sounds, none of it involves translation errors since, as I mentioned, *Mary, Jesus* and *Christ* are just Greek ways of expressing Jewish names and concepts—and God gave us the New Testament in Greek to bring it most efficiently to the ancient world. The problem is the Church's severing of its Jewish roots, thus forgetting the Jewishness of these names and concepts.

Things get even murkier when we realize some major mistranslations lurk in virtually all our English versions of the Bible, leading to serious misconceptions. Think of the name *Jacob*. What comes to mind when you hear that name? Probably things like *Israel, patriarch, Old Testament*. What about *James?* You think of *Christian, epistle, brother of Jesus*. The disconnect between the two is large. Just imagine referring to *Abraham, Isaac* and

173

*James!* It almost sounds like we are mixing two religions, Judaism and Christianity, doesn't it?

But did you know that what our English Bibles call the epistle of James is actually the epistle of Jacob? And did you know that English is the only language in the world where *Jacob* in the New Testament is translated "James"?[21] It does not take a Greek scholar to see that the original text says *Yakobus,* "Jacob," and not "James" or any form thereof. In German Bibles, for instance, the epistle is called *Jakobus;* in French, it is *Jacques;* in Japanese, it is *Yakobu;* in Polish, it is *Jakub.* Only our English Bibles say "James"—completely without justification.[22] Yet words and names have meanings and conjure up images of all kinds.

Let's look at the opening verse of this epistle as rendered in The New International Version: "James, a servant of God and of the Lord Jesus Christ, to the twelve tribes scattered among the nations: Greetings" (James 1:1). You might take this as saying, "This is the Christian leader James writing to Christians scattered around the world, figuratively referred to as the twelve tribes."

But what if we rendered the Greek literally, also rendering other names in a way that reflects their Hebrew/Aramaic background?[23] It would sound like this: "Jacob, a servant of God and of the Lord Yeshua the Messiah, to the twelve tribes scattered among the nations: Shalom." Now what comes to mind? It sounds like a letter from a Jewish believer in the Messiah to Jewish believers scattered around the world. And notice that one key word: *Jewish.* The New Testament is a Jewish book! (Pastors, if you really want to start a revolution in your churches, tell your congregants to "turn to the epistle of Jacob" the next time you preach, or make reference to "Jacob, the leader of the congregation in Jerusalem." You will certainly stir some things up!)

174

Let's take this one step further: The Greek word *syn-agoges*, meaning "assembly, meeting place, synagogue," occurs 56 times in the Greek New Testament, being found most frequently in the gospels and Acts (53 times). Obviously when you hear the word *synagogue* you think *Jewish*.

In the gospels Jesus frequently attended the local synagogues, where He often found Himself in conflict with the Jewish leadership.[24] This makes sense to us, since Jesus had not yet died on the cross and founded Christianity, so, we think, it was okay for Him to attend synagogue, right? Most of us see Paul's evangelistic work in Acts in the same way, wrongly thinking that Paul, a converted Jew, went into the synagogues to preach Christianity to the unconverted Jews, right? And how is *synagoges* translated each of these 53 times in the gospels and Acts? "Synagogue," of course.[25]

The word also occurs twice in the book of Revelation, speaking of those who claim to be Jews and are not, but are a *synagoges* of Satan (2:9 and 3:9). Once more, translators render the word as "synagogue"—this time a Jewish synagogue of Satan (naturally, since the context is negative!).[26] So, 55 out of 56 times, *synagoges* is translated "synagogue," indicating that there is not much dispute about the meaning of the word.

Only once in our English Bibles is *synagoges* not translated "synagogue"—in James 2:2: "Suppose a man comes into your *meeting* [or, in the King James Version, *assembly*] . . ." (emphasis added). What a revelation! Since this is a "Christian" context rather than a "Jewish" context, *synagoges* cannot possibly mean "synagogue." Rather, it has to mean "meeting" or "assembly," since Christians do not meet in synagogues. This is confirmed by James 5:14, where those who are sick are enjoined to call for "the elders of *the church*" (emphasis added).

There is only one problem with this line of reasoning: This is the epistle of Jacob, not James, and it was written to Jewish Christians, not Gentile Christians. That is why David Stern in his *Jewish New Testament* rightly renders this, "Suppose a man comes into your synagogue," while Kenneth Wuest's *Expanded Translation* reads, "For if there comes into your synagogue [the meeting place of Christian-Jews]." As New Testament scholar Craig Keener commented, the word translated "'Assembly' (KJV, NASB, NRSV) or 'meeting' (NIV, TEV) is literally 'synagogue,' either because James wants the whole Jewish community to embrace his example, or because the Jewish-Christian congregations (cf. 5:14) also considered themselves messianic synagogues."[27] The latter explanation is most likely.[28]

How novel this sounds to most Christian ears—a Jewish epistle written to Jewish believers who met in messianic synagogues. But that is clearly what James 2:2 indicates, although it is not the way most Christian teachers have interpreted the text. Rather, they have turned it upside down. The explanation of nineteenth-century Christian commentator Albert Barnes makes this clear:

> **For if there come into your assembly**—Margin, as in Greek, "synagogue." It is remarkable that this is the only place in the New Testament where the word "synagogue" is applied to the Christian church. It is probably employed here because the apostle was writing to those who had been Jews; and it is to be presumed that the word synagogue would be naturally used by the early converts from Judaism to designate a Christian place of worship, or a Christian congregation, and it was probably so employed until it was superseded by a word which the Gentile converts would be more likely to employ, and which would, in fact, be better and more expressive—the word church.[29]

Notice those two key phrases: "the apostle was writing to those who had been Jews" and "the word synagogue would be naturally used by the early converts from Judaism to designate a Christian place of worship." So when a Jew follows Yeshua the Jewish Messiah, he is no longer a Jew but rather a convert from Judaism to Christianity! What a bizarre concept—yet a concept quite common in Christian circles worldwide. It is reflected again in Barnes' closing comment that the word *church* superseded the word *synagogue* due to the influx of Gentile converts. This says a lot.

In light of all this, I ask you: Am I overstating things when I say that in terms of the restoration of Jewish roots, we desperately need a revolution in the Church? In certain ways this revolution will challenge the very meaning of *church*. We are not speaking of a new and different religion but rather the realization of what was spoken by the prophets of Israel. In other words, *church* is not so much a word introduced by Jesus to describe all Christians around the globe as it is the Lord's way of designating His worldwide congregation, His community of faith from every nation, consisting of Jew and Gentile alike, bound together through Yeshua the Messiah and King.

When He said in Matthew 16:18, "I will build my church, and the gates of Hades [hell] will not overcome it," He was not speaking to His Jewish disciples about a new religious body and a new religion. To the contrary, the Greek word ekklesia, translated "church" in our English Bibles, simply meant "congregation, assembly of believers," as we pointed out in chapter 3. The Jewish translators of the Septuagint (the Greek translation of the Hebrew Bible made more than two hundred years before Jesus) used this word to render the Hebrew words qahal and edah, both meaning "congregation, community, assembly." And since Jesus/Yeshua spoke to His dis-

177

ciples in either Hebrew or Aramaic, He would have made reference to building His qahal/edah or qehala'/kenishta'—standard words for already-known concepts.[30]

What *was* new in the declaration of Jesus—radically new—was that this community would be *His* community ("I will build *My* congregation"), consisting of redeemed Jews and Gentiles, all with equal access to God, all with equal rights, all cleansed in Messiah's blood, all empowered by the Spirit, all sent to change the world. What a congregation! No wonder the gates of hell cannot prevail against it.

A restoration of Jewish roots would also emphasize the importance of concepts like the Kingdom of God, a major theme in Acts but hardly one in most evangelical circles today. Yet according to Acts 1:3, "After his suffering, he showed himself to these men and gave many convincing proofs that he was alive. *He appeared to them over a period of forty days and spoke about the kingdom of God*" (emphasis added). What does this signify?[31] What did He speak of during that forty-day period?

Philip "preached the good news of the kingdom of God and the name of Jesus Christ" to the Samaritans, who believed and were baptized (Acts 8:12). Paul and Barnabas told the believers in Antioch, "We must go through many hardships to enter the kingdom of God" (14:22). In Ephesus "Paul entered the synagogue and spoke boldly there for three months, arguing persuasively about the kingdom of God" (19:8), and in his closing address to the elders there said, "Now I know that none of you among whom I have gone about preaching the kingdom will ever see me again" (20:25). In Rome he met with other Jewish leaders, and "from morning till evening he explained and declared to them the kingdom of God and tried to convince them about Jesus from the Law of Moses and from the Prophets" (28:23). In fact, the closing verse of Acts, speaking of Paul's activity, says, "Boldly and without hindrance he preached the kingdom of God and taught about the Lord Jesus Christ" (28:31).

Jesus, Philip, Paul and Barnabas were not merely talking about future prophetic schemes or abstract spiritual concepts.[32] At the least, based on everything we read in the Scriptures up to the book of Acts, they were talking about the breaking in of God's Kingdom through the Messiah's coming (didn't Jesus announce the arrival of the Kingdom during His earthly ministry?), along with the expansion of this Kingdom and its eventual domination of the earth (as we pray in the Lord's Prayer).[33] This has implications for daily living, for ministry in the gifts and power of the Spirit, for our view of the end times. And didn't Jesus tell us to seek first God's Kingdom and righteousness, and then our earthly needs would be met (Matthew 6:33; see also Romans 14:17)?

A restoration of Jewish roots would also give us a better grasp on some of the end-time spiritual conflicts, not least of which is the battle for Jerusalem, the only city Scripture commands us to pray for (Psalm 122:6; Isaiah 62:1–8), the only city God called the apple of His eye, which He promised to protect with a wall of fire (Zechariah 2:5), the only city over which it is recorded that Jesus wept (Luke 19:41) and the only city of which it is written that all nations will attack it and God Himself will fight for it (Zechariah 12:1–9).

This is because Jerusalem is *the* city to which Yeshua will return (Zechariah 14:1–5) and the city that must welcome Him back. He will not return to this earth until His own people, represented by the Jewish city of Jerusalem, welcome Him back (see Matthew 23:37).[34] Everything is hanging on Jerusalem. That is why the conflict over this city is so great. That is why the terrorist group

179

Hamas has freely spoken of "the Battle for Jerusalem," proclaiming that "Jerusalem will be the battlefield" and pledging, "Revolution until victory!"[35]

Think of it. Jerusalem is not mentioned a single time in the Koran, it has never been a major attraction for Islamic pilgrims, and Muslims living near Jerusalem pray daily with their *backs* toward the city (while religious Jews worldwide pray facing Jerusalem), yet the whole Muslim world wants Jerusalem to be the capital of a Palestinian state. Why? The capital city of every sovereign nation is recognized by all other nations, with the sole exception of Jerusalem, *the* holy city of the Jewish people for the last three thousand years, and the chosen capital of the nation of Israel. Why?

And why is it that in the year 2001, Christian leaders representing church organizations ranging from Catholic to American Baptist to Anglican to United Methodist to Reformed Church of America to African Methodist Episcopal to Evangelical Lutheran to Korean Presbyterian to Greek Orthodox to Mennonite to Moravian to National Council of the Churches of Christ in the U.S.A. (and more!) wrote to Secretary of State Colin Powell and urged him *not* to recognize Jerusalem as Israel's capital at this time? "We tremble to consider the destructive consequences that would follow the premature moving, as called for by Congress, of the U.S. embassy from Tel Aviv to Jerusalem."[36] I tremble to read these words!

And to think that these leaders primarily blamed the Israelis for the ongoing violence in the land, despite the fact that most Israelis long for a peaceful settlement with the Palestinians (while Palestinian children's textbooks call for Israel's annihilation, Palestinian summer camps train children how to kill Jews, and Palestinian universities celebrate suicide bombings); despite the fact that Israel grants religious freedom to Palestinians (while Palestinian Muslims have tortured and killed their own

180

people who have become Christians), and despite the fact that the Israeli government has not once initiated the cycle of violence during times of peace (while the Palestinian government ordered a death sentence for any of their people selling their land to Jews).[37]

Is it of no significance to us that Palestinians danced in the streets of their cities on September 11, 2001, while Israel declared a day of mourning? Is it of no meaning that the Mufti of Jerusalem (the Muslim spiritual leader, sponsored by the Palestinian Authority) has not only called for the destruction of the Jews but even denies the Holocaust? Only a Church that had lost sight of her Jewish roots could so vocally side against Israel.[38]

Christian pacifist author Dale Brown once commented that "the radical must be a man of tradition, for without roots 'he is unlikely to have the security to question to the depths.'"[39] This holds true for the Church's Jewish roots. A proper grounding in our biblical foundations would make us secure enough to question many of the man-made traditions that have often undermined the Word.

Sometimes the most radical, revolutionary thing we can do is return to our roots. Sometimes the way to real progress involves going back and retrieving what was lost before moving forward into unexplored territory. Sometimes the most revolutionary thing we can do is tear down and repair before trying to build something new. But doing this is costly, painful and quite unsettling.

My question for you is this: Do you really have a choice?

181

# 11

# Going Outside the Camp

> God always reserved a seed for himself; a few that worshipped in spirit and in truth. I have often doubted, whether these were not the very persons whom the rich and honourable Christians, who will always have number as well as power on their side, did not stigmatize, from time to time, with the title of heretics.
>
> John Wesley
> from his sermon "The Wisdom of God's Counsels"

To organized opposition he [Jesus] responds with the formal founding of a new social reality. New teachings are no threat, as long as the teacher stands alone; a movement, extending his personality in both time and space, presenting an alternative to the structures that

182

were there before, challenges the system as no mere words ever could.

John Howard Yoder, *The Politics of Jesus*

A man who starts changing the system is dangerous. . . . When a man starts shaking up the religious, political, and social system, the people *in* the system feel that they have to stop him.

Tom Skinner, *Words of Revolution*

Do you see what this means—all these pioneers who blazed the way, all these veterans cheering us on? It means we'd better get on with it. . . . Keep your eyes on Jesus, who both began and finished this race we're in. . . . He never lost sight of where He was headed—that exhilarating finish in and with God—He could put up with anything along the way: cross, shame, whatever. And now He's THERE, in the place of honor, right alongside God. . . .

Hebrews 12:1ff., MESSAGE

In 1998, German evangelist Ulrich Parzany received a medal for his outstanding youth work in Germany. In his response he said: "They crucified my boss, Jesus Christ. I am being honoured. What did I do wrong?"

Wolfgang Simson, *Houses That Change the World*

In the spring of 1983, I sat in a friend's home with a small group of hungry and hurting believers, praying and seeking the Lord together. We had been part of a wonderful, life-transforming move of the Spirit in the previous months, an outpouring that seemed to have the potential of touching thousands of people. But division and sin in our church cut short the move of God, and rather than fight with the other leaders, a number of us wrote letters of resignation, stepped down from our positions and left.

We could not believe that, yet again, things had gotten messed up, and we wondered out loud to one another, "Will the Church ever get things right, or will there have to be a whole new expression of the Body, an expression that would focus only on small house meetings without formal leadership or structure?"

One of the older men there had been burned by his prior church experience in a very serious way, not once but two or three times. It seemed that "the system," by its very nature, was doomed to failure. And so this dear brother made a simple, matter-of-fact statement that reflected our sentiments at that time: "The organized Church has failed."

For a moment it seemed as if he was right, as if God had another plan—and in our minds, this almost meant a complete retreat from church as we knew it. Several in the group even envisioned some kind of holy gathering in an obscure location where we could build our own end-time community of believers. We were ready to go for it!

Yet within a few weeks God convicted us and showed us that we were overreacting and in danger of heading toward spiritual elitism. In fact, to our dismay and disappointment, He clearly called us to become part of another, somewhat typical local church, working together with the leader there. Looking back almost twenty years later, I have no doubt that this was the will of God.[1]

You see, the Lord *does* have a people on the earth today, and it is not limited to a select few groups scattered in isolated places on the planet. He is working in and through denominations, He is working in and through mega-churches, He is working in and through traditional churches, He is even working in and through

184

gospel radio and TV (although the mixture there can be quite extreme).

It is an error to reject what Jesus has accepted, even if He has accepted it only in part, and to deem as unworthy something He Himself favors with His presence, even if that presence does not represent His fullness. It is an error to develop the Elijah complex that says, "I alone remain faithful to the Lord!" It is also an error to disqualify a church or group or denomination because of some obvious flaws, even if some of its practices do more harm than good. We must be careful here!

But that does not mean things are anywhere near the way they are supposed to be or that we should accept the status quo or that the boat does not need to be rocked. Far from it! Much in "the system" must be confronted and changed—quite drastically at that. There is a desperate need for a revolution in the Church, especially in the West, and that means taking revolutionary action. But as I stated at the outset of this book, *revolution*, rightly understood, is a very disturbing word.

It is one thing to affirm that God is working within all kinds of groups, structures and settings, and that He is active within "the system." But that does not mean He wants us to let the system go unchallenged or that He will not call us to leave the system. He might very well lead us to march to the beat of a different drummer, and that means being out of step with many others.

And so I warn you: Following your convictions will prove costly. Following the moving of the Spirit—remember, He is not standing still—will mean much agony in intercession and stretching of the soul. Following your Master closely will mean crucifixion, rejection, reproach and shame.

Most of the opposition you experience will come from brothers and sisters in the Lord, from fellow workers and friends. It will come from "the mainstream," from those who are "sound in the faith," from those who are "established in the truth," even from those who are "on fire for the Lord." Often it will come from those whose acceptance you value.

Yet that is the path of obedience, the price of being a pioneer. Who among us will make the break? Will you? What price must you pay to be fully faithful to the Lord? What will He require of you?

If your traditions stifle the Word of God, why adhere to the traditions? Is it not clear by now that those traditions will not change or go away by themselves? If your structure stands in the way of the Spirit, why remain loyal to the structure? It has been here longer than you have, and if not challenged it will remain here long after you are gone. Why expect a metamorphosis in the establishment now? If your spiritual-political alliances keep you from fulfilling your calling, why maintain the carnal bond? Why perpetuate the sham?

I once spoke to a friend who, together with his wife, had served his denomination for more than thirty years. They had been home missionaries as well as foreign missionaries, often living sacrificially for the good of the work. Yet they were very frustrated with the organization's policies, calling them controlling, hindering and stifling. In fact, neither this man nor his wife had a single good thing to say about the denomination they represented. Their attitude was even marked by disdain.

"Then why do you stay with them?" I asked him. "Why not work with others?"

"All my contacts are within the denomination," he replied. "All my financial support comes from them. Where would I go?" Outside the camp!

Why remain handcuffed to a system and handicapped by a system that is not going to change? And why dishonor the system by staying loyal to it on paper while expressing disrespect and even scorn for its leaders and policies? How can that be right in the sight of God?

Sadly I remembered having a similar conversation with this devoted brother more than fifteen years before; and now, more than a decade and a half later, his frustrations with the denomination were greater and his disagreements deeper. Still, it was next to impossible for him to make the break. This does *not* have to be your story, too.

One day you and I will stand before the Judge of all the earth and give an account for our lives. What will we say when He asks us why we failed to do what we knew was right, why the affirmation of man was more important to us than the affirmation of heaven, why we willingly deceived ourselves with cheap answers rather than walk the costly path of submission to the Father's will? How will we respond?

Leaders in particular cannot take this lightly, as Paul warns clearly and without exaggeration:

If any man builds on this foundation [of Jesus Christ] using gold, silver, costly stones, wood, hay or straw, his work will be shown for what it is, because the Day will bring it to light. It will be revealed with fire, and the fire will test the quality of each man's work. If what he has built survives, he will receive his reward. If it is burned up, he will suffer loss; he himself will be saved, but only as one escaping through the flames.

1 Corinthians 3:12–15

What a thought! The work we have done will be shown for what it really is, revealed by fire and tested by fire. Much of it, representing the labor of a lifetime, will not even survive. How then should we lead? How then should we live? If what we are building will not stand the test, why labor in vain?

187

When we stand face to face with eternal reality, stripped of every pretense and excuse, how will we deny the fact that the desire for self-preservation drove us to save our lives through compromise rather than lose our lives through obedience? What will we say when confronted with the fact that our concern for financial security overruled the voice of the Spirit, and our insistence on keeping social ties intact muted the Word of God?

How will we explain our strange belief that it was right and acceptable for Jesus and the apostles to suffer and be rejected (not to mention the persecuted Church worldwide in every century) while *we* escape without conflict and pain? How will we justify our position that we wanted resurrection without crucifixion, glory without reproach, and revolution without upheaval and pain?

Jesus suffered disgrace and rejection at the hands of His own people, the people of the Book, the people of the covenant—and we are called to follow His example. As Scripture states:

> The high priest carries the blood of animals into the Most Holy Place as a sin offering, but the bodies are burned outside the camp. And so Jesus also suffered outside the city gate to make the people holy through his own blood. Let us, then, go to him outside the camp, bearing the disgrace he bore. For here we do not have an enduring city, but we are looking for the city that is to come.

Hebrews 13:11–14

Yes, following Jesus means going outside the camp—even though the camp is familiar to us, even though the camp is where our roots have been, even though the camp has been our place of security. Going outside the camp means bearing the disgrace Jesus bore—and that disgrace

188

comes first and foremost from established religion. Yet, as He bore it, pioneers must bear it, too.

Remember that Hebrews was written to Jewish believers in Yeshua the Messiah, and there was constant pressure on them to go back to their old way of life, a theme addressed in virtually every chapter of the epistle. The old way seemed so sacred with its priesthood and Temple, so ancient with its time-honored traditions, so stable with its long, respected pedigree. Yet the new and better way had come, and that meant making a break from the established way with its beautiful buildings and prestige, even though it seemed to have history on its side.[2]

Leaving that camp brings disgrace and reproach, but that is the price of being a pioneer. There is no other way. And without pioneers there can be no dynamic change, no taking of new ground, no revolution.

We can gain some insight into all this by looking at the dialogue between the Jewish blind man, healed by Jesus, and the Jewish religious leadership, steeped in their traditions. The blind man had met God firsthand; the leaders relied on a divine encounter dating back generations. The results of the conflict were inevitable:

They asked him, "What did he do to you? How did he open your eyes?" He answered, "I have told you already and you did not listen. Why do you want to hear it again? Do you want to become his disciples, too?" Then they hurled insults at him and said, "You are this fellow's disciple! We are disciples of Moses! We know that God spoke to Moses, but as for this fellow, we don't even know where he comes from." The man answered, "Now that is remarkable! You don't know where he comes from, yet he opened my eyes. We know that God does not listen to sinners. He listens to the godly man who does his will. Nobody has ever heard of opening the eyes of a man born blind. If this man were not from God, he could do nothing." To this they replied, "You were steeped in sin at birth; how dare you lecture us!" And they threw him out.

John 9:26–34

Notice first that when the healed man suggested sarcastically that the leaders might be interested in becoming disciples of Yeshua, they hurled insults at him: "We are disciples of Moses! We are part of a proven religious tradition dating back millennia. Why should we follow this unknown upstart?"

And when he revealed the folly of their position—they were actually hardening their hearts against a visitation of the God whom they claimed to serve and honor—they turned on him viciously: " 'You were steeped in sin at birth; how dare you lecture us!' And they threw him out"—outside the camp, outside the borders of traditional religion, outside the place of earthly security.[3]

And it was there, outside the camp, that Jesus found him, as John 9:35 records: "Jesus heard that they had thrown him out, and when he found him, he said, 'Do you believe in the Son of Man?' " Jesus will find you there, too! In fact, it is the place where the Lord Himself can be found. In the words of Hebrews: "Let us, then, *go to him* outside the camp, bearing the disgrace he bore" (emphasis added). Jesus is outside the camp, too, and it is allegiance to Him that brings us out.

Yet for many it is difficult to leave the security of the camp and the safety of the fold, whether that fold is a denomination, an independent congregation, a small house church or even a family tradition. Anything can become part of "the establishment," part of that which resists biblical change, part of "the system." But the fold promises safety, and many believe that staying within the camp guarantees protection from deception, error

190

and spiritual attack. Thus it is fear that often holds us back, and nothing paralyzes like fear.

Many leaders exploit this fear, sometimes out of pure motives and with real sincerity, seeking to protect the flock from perceived danger, and at other times out of selfishness and pride, not wanting to see their influence diminished. This, too, needs to be challenged. As Frank Viola explains,

> The concept goes something like this: everyone must answer to someone else who is in a higher ecclesiastical position. In the garden-variety, post-war evangelical church, this translates into the "laypeople" answering to the pastor. In turn, the pastor must answer to a person who has more authority.
>
> So the pastor will typically trace his accountability to a denominational headquarters, to another church (often called the "mother church"), or to an influential Christian worker (who is perceived to have a higher rank in the ecclesiastical pyramid). As a result, the "laypeople" are said to be "covered" by the pastor, and the pastor is said to be "covered" by the denomination, the mother church, or the Christian worker. The fact that people can trace their accountability to a higher ecclesiastical authority is the equivalent of being protected by that authority (so the thinking goes).
>
> But this line of thinking generates the following telling questions: Who covers the mother church? Who covers the denominational headquarters? And who covers the Christian worker? Some have offered the pat answer that *God* covers these "higher" authorities. But such an answer begs the question; for why can't God be the covering for the "laypeople," or even the pastor? Of course, the real problem with the "God-denominational-clergy-laity" model goes far beyond the incoherent, pretzel logic to which it leads. The chief problem is that it violates the spirit of the NT; for behind the pious rhetoric of "providing accountability" and "having a covering," there

looms a system of government that is bereft of Biblical support and driven by a spirit of control.[4]

Certainly, not all of this is what Viola calls "pious rhetoric," nor is all of it "driven by a spirit of control." If God has genuinely raised up leaders to shepherd the flock, giving them insight into the needs of the sheep, then it is right for the sheep to submit to their authority and wrong for them to break away every time a conflict emerges. Accountability, rightly understood, brings health; and covenantal relationships, when mutually embraced, provide safety.

But Viola is right in exposing the myth of the supernatural protection of the covering (or "the camp"), since the covering (or camp) cannot guarantee orthodoxy of faith and practice but only uniformity. In other words, Baptist denominations believe Pentecostal denominations are in doctrinal error with regard to the gifts of the Spirit, while Pentecostal denominations believe Baptist denominations are in doctrinal error with regard to "once saved always saved"—to name just two areas of divergence. How then does staying within either of those denominations guarantee doctrinal accuracy? It does not. It guarantees doctrinal harmony only for those within their particular group. Yet this pressure toward uniformity and harmony is what holds many of us back. We must wholeheartedly reject this pressure!

In reality, denominational churches can have as much doctrinal error as independent churches; house meetings can be just as ineffective as liturgical services; and groups that have been around for years can be just as deluded as groups formed yesterday. Yet believers are held captive by the fear that leaving their group or organization or denomination or fellowship or church will make them vulnerable to the attacks of the enemy and leave them wide open to deception and error.[5]

/ But what if there is deception and error in the group they are leaving? Being part of a group—especially an older, established group—is no guarantee of biblical truth. And staying with the old organization does not necessarily lessen the spiritual attack. Often the old attacks were worse!

To state it again: "The system" thrives on *uniformity*, which is then called *orthodoxy*; and thus, by circular reasoning, those within the system are considered orthodox and thought to be protected from heresy. How absurd! There is no biblical support for this position, nor is it even logical.

Of course, leaving the Body of Christ as a whole and breaking off from all fellowship is both dangerous and contrary to the Word (see Hebrews 10:25). And, without a doubt, rejecting all authority in your life and having no spiritual leadership to whom you relate makes you *very* vulnerable and leaves you dreadfully exposed. Your very attitude is an invitation to demonic forces.

But for most of you reading this book, that is not the problem. (If it is a problem, stay submitted where you are until you nail your independence and self-will to the cross.) Most of you have wrestled with scriptural questions for years, wondering why the teachings of the New Testament seem so unrelated to the Church of today, finding yourself increasingly eager to become part of a fellowship of believers who will just go for it. You want to throw yourself *into* something even more than you want to get *out* of something, and week after week, as you sit through service after service (or as you *lead* service after service), you ask yourself, "Is this it? Is this the faith for which Jesus died? Is this everything God has? Isn't there more?"

My friend, those questions are prompted by the Spirit. They are indications of a heart after God, a heart that yearns for divine reality, a heart that wants to obey at any cost. They are not the marks of rebellion and pride. You know you would joyfully serve and submit if only you could find some leaders worthy of your trust, along with a congregation willing to take the plunge.[6]

I tell you again, that is where Jesus is, calling you to follow Him, promising to meet you there. But I also tell you again that following this Man Jesus, the Jesus of the Scriptures, is no easy thing, especially in twenty-first-century America. Following Him is dangerous to the flesh and deadly to earthly reputations. Following Him is *unsettling*.

Consider the penetrating words of Danish philosopher Søren Kierkegaard. Our Pioneer paid quite a price!

> Lest we forget, it was not some petty squabble between Christ and the world that put Christ on the cross. No, love of God is hatred of the world. And the day when Christianity and the world become friends—yes, then Christianity is abolished. Then Christ will have to be judged for being only a dreamer, a fanatic. If he had not been so intolerant, he would have gotten on quite well with the world and with its religious authorities; he would then not have been put to death, something that would have been totally unnecessary. Instead, he would have become someone great, or at least much appreciated, just as his followers eventually became when the Church triumphed—an occurrence that indeed makes a lie of the saying that the pupil is not above the teacher.[7]

Yet somehow, for the Church in the West, it would seem that the pupil *is* above his Teacher and the servant *is* above his Master. We are not treated as He was! But this is not because the world has changed, nor is it because the Master Teacher has changed. It is because we have changed.

Consider carefully the testimony of the Word of God. In his second letter to Timothy, Paul reminded his younger

disciple about the things he had endured for the Kingdom: "You, however, know all about my teaching, my way
of life, my purpose, faith, patience, love, endurance, persecutions, sufferings—what kinds of things happened to
me in Antioch, Iconium and Lystra, the persecutions I
endured. Yet the Lord rescued me from all of them" (2 Timothy 3:10–11).

But this was not Paul's lot alone. Quite the contrary,
it was the expected lot of all who followed the Lord. As
he wrote, "In fact, everyone who wants to live a godly
life in Christ Jesus will be persecuted" (2 Timothy 3:12).
Everyone!

The persecuted Church worldwide understands these
verses well, without the need for commentary or expo-
sition. Their own lives are the commentary. Yet for the
Church in the West, verses such as these, which occur
throughout the New Testament, seem foreign, distant,
strange.[8] Why? Because we are so much like the world
that we do not merit the world's persecution; because
Satan's people are doing a far better job of making saints
into sinners than we are at making sinners into saints;
because hell's evangelistic strategies are employed with
far greater zeal than are the evangelistic strategies of
our Lord. This is tragic but undeniably true—at least
here in the West.

Brother Andrew, the fearless leader of Open Doors
Ministries, once met with a Romanian pastor who had
just been released from prison.[9] This pastor, who had
been tortured for his faith, knew very little about the
state of the Church in the free world, so he asked
Brother Andrew, whose native country was Holland,
how the pastors there coped with persecution and
imprisonment.

Brother Andrew explained to him that the Christian
leaders in his country were not being persecuted or
imprisoned for their faith. This drew an incredulous

response from the pastor. "How then do you explain 2 Timothy 3:12?" he asked.

Although this verse was well known to Brother Andrew, the reference itself did not ring a bell, so he opened his Bible and turned to it, reading the words afresh: "In fact, everyone who wants to live a godly life in Christ Jesus will be persecuted." He then looked at the Romanian pastor and said, "I'm so sorry." What else could he say?

In the Netherlands today, homosexual marriages are sanctioned, gay couples can adopt their own children, prostitution is legal and unionized, and marijuana can be bought openly in "coffee shops." The Church is so superficial and traditional that, although most Dutch people would consider themselves Christians, the born-again population of the country is probably less than two percent.

To drive this point home, let me relate something that happened to a team of graduates from FIRE School of Ministry who were ministering in the Netherlands in 2001. They were shocked to see a poster of an attractive, topless young woman on the classroom wall of a "Christian" school. When one of our grads asked the teacher why a pornographic picture was on the wall, his explanation was even more shocking than the poster itself: The young woman pictured was the "Mary" of the month, part of an effort by the Catholic Church to stimulate interest in religion, with a new topless Mary planned for every month of the year.

God is my witness that every word of this account is accurate. Yet in the midst of such a society, true believers are not persecuted. How can this be?

The situation in America is even more perplexing. One-third of Americans attend church services every week, half attend church services every month and more than forty percent claim to have had a life-changing experience with Jesus. As of 2001, there were multiplied

thousands congregations in our country with member-
ships of more than one thousand. Yet we are one of the
most worldly, carnal, sensual, materialistic nations on
earth. In fact, one reason much of the Muslim world
hates us so much, aside from our stand with Israel, is
that we are experts at exporting sin worldwide.

I have heard American Christian leaders say that
many Muslims hate America because our country funds
ninety percent of missionary work around the globe.
But that is hardly true, regardless of how much fund-
ing of the Gospel we actually do. The opposite is true.

Travel the nations of the world. Here and there you
will see evidence of Gospel work funded by the United
States, if you see it at all. But everywhere you will find
evidence of our decadent culture: The worst American
TV shows are aired worldwide, along with the most sensual and violent American films, including pornogra-
phy galore, not to mention MTV in its distinctive Asian
and European forms. Even rap music, replete with vile
content and vulgarities, can be heard in languages like
Japanese, German and Hebrew—all thanks to the good
old U.S.A. And what kind of impact has materialism,
the worst of the "isms," had on the nations? In this, too,
America leads the way.[10]

How then do we explain the fact that America boasts
so much Christianity yet remains so morally dark? It is
because the light within us is darkness. As I have stated
repeatedly through the years, America is in such poor
condition today because the Church of America is in such
poor condition. "Christianity" is everywhere around us
(in more traditional forms, this is true in Europe as well),
yet when it is weighed in the balance, it is found lacking.

And herein lies the trap: The apparent success of the
Gospel, be it in our national heritage or in our contemporary society, has tempered our radicality and kept us
within the confines of the camp. If we were missionar-

ies in a Buddhist or Hindu society, we would not expect the acceptance of the system, nor would we claim the rights of the privileged majority. From the outset we would find ourselves outside the established camp, rejected and misunderstood just as our Savior was, seeking to bring about change by the power of the Gospel, whatever the cost.

But in America and Europe our mentality is different. After all, we belong to "Christian" nations with a long and rich "Christian" history. We dare not go too far lest we disqualify ourselves. We dare not be too radical lest we become irrelevant. We dare not leave the camp. And by thinking like this, we deceive ourselves.

We *do* need a spiritual revolution, but everywhere around us are pacifying influences cooling our passion, dimming our vision, blurring our perceptions, dulling our convictions. Everywhere around us are voices saying, "Accept the status quo," while deep down in our hearts we know that Jesus came to overthrow the status quo.

How else do we explain His words in Luke 12:49–51, presented with biting vigor in *The Message*?

> "I've come to start a fire on this earth—how I wish it were blazing right now! I've come to change everything, turn everything rightside up—how I long for it to be finished! Do you think I came to smooth things over and make everything nice? Not so. I've come to disrupt and confront!"

That is how our Lord responds to that which is wrong: He seeks to make it right. And that means conflict and misunderstanding. Yet we seek to smooth things over and make everything nice. How contrary this is to the Jesus pattern! (Once again I add this caution: Following the Jesus pattern means acting in humility, coming as a servant rather than a boss, walking in grace and longsuffering, overcoming evil with good, honoring authority and living in peace as much as it lies with you, and losing your life rather than saving it. It does not give you or me the right to be nasty, contentious or obnoxious. But it does call us to be advocates of radical change regardless of the cost or consequences.)

When Kierkegaard wrote his scathing indictments against "the triumphant Church" of his day, we must remember that he lived at a time when almost the entire institutional Church in his country was apostate, having very little in common with the Church of the New Testament. Yet his words remain hauntingly relevant:

> The triumphant Church, or established Christianity, resembles the Church militant no more than a square resembles a circle. It would be utterly impossible for the first Christians to recognize Christianity in its current distortion. Yes, they would hear Christianity preached and hear that what was said was entirely true, but to their great horror they would see that the actual conditions for being a Christian are exactly the opposite of what they were in their day. To be a Christian now is no more like being a Christian in their day than walking on one's legs is like walking on one's head.[11]

To use another image, for years we have been trying to get the car to fly—giving it a new paint job, putting on new tires, replacing the engine, even changing its name. But a car cannot fly regardless of how much work we put into it. It needs to be redesigned with wings! The engineers need to follow the blueprints for a plane, not an automobile, since the vehicle needs revolutionary change, not just minor modifications. Only then can it fly.

199

That is what we are saying about the Church. There must be revolutionary change. The biblical blueprints must be followed. Minor modifications and improvements will not produce the desired results—and the desired results are beyond our expectations and dreams.

In that sense I do believe in the triumphant Church—meaning that the working of the Spirit worldwide will produce a massive harvest of souls and a glorious Bride set apart for the Son. But in another sense it is the apparent triumph of the Church that holds us back, slowing down our progress, tempering our radicality and arguing for balance rather than obedience. Jesus calls us to be militant.

Our "boasting" says it all. Unlike Paul, who boasted in his sufferings for Jesus, most of us can boast only of our accomplishments. The contemporary American Church has stars instead of scars and performers instead of prisoners, and we measure our success by high ratings rather than by hard beatings. When the world embraces us we are glad. But Jesus and the apostles considered such embraces nothing less than Satan's treachery, to be avoided like the plague.

The disciples in China can teach us something about this, too. Long ago the Communist government there established a nationally accepted church body called the Three Self Church. It is perfectly legal and out in the open; it has its own buildings and even some Bibles it can distribute. But it cannot preach against the government, it cannot preach on controversial political themes and it cannot preach the Lordship of Jesus in a way that would conflict with the Communist system. And so it exists without persecution.

Being a member of the Three Self Church will not cost you your life, nor will it cost you a prison sentence, a beating or even your job. Yet the vast majority of China's true Christians refuse to be associated with the

Three Self Church, preferring instead to go outside the camp with Jesus, suffering shame, harassment, imprisonment, torture and even death.

In August 2001 the United Nations held a convention of world religions, drawing protests from some quarters because the Dalai Lama was not invited (out of deference to Communist China), while others protested because evangelical Chinese Christians, persecuted fiercely in their country, were not invited to be part of the Christian delegation.

What was the official response?

> "The Chinese constitution has explicit provisions," said the Rev. Cao Shengjie, Vice President of the China Christian Council and a member of the delegation. "If you carry out normal religious activities, no one interferes." But she added that religious activities that interrupt the daily stability of Chinese life or that place Chinese people in danger are "considered an offense and will be disciplined by law."[12]

That statement says it all: "Normal religious activities" are accepted by the world and by dead religion, but anything that interrupts the stability of daily life constitutes an offense and will be disciplined by law. Following Jesus interrupts the stability of daily life! Biblical obedience threatens established religion! But "the camp" does not tolerate dissent—and so Jesus remains outside the camp, still bearing disgrace and reproach, still waiting for us there.

On the one hand, that place outside the camp is a place of glory, of divine habitation, of spiritual vitality, of holy power, a place inhabited by multitudes of God's people. On the other hand, it is a place of challenge and confrontation, a place that is often lonely and painful, a place that will be small before it is large, rejected before it is honored and scorned before it is respected. Will we follow Jesus there?

Will we be true pioneers, following our scriptural convictions and the clear leading of the Spirit, even if others call us crazy? D. L. Moody was known as "Crazy Moody" early in his Christian work, whereas today his highly respected name is associated with a Bible institute, a Christian magazine, a publishing organization and other Kingdom works. We cannot have all the success first! If we do, it is unlikely that we have fully carried the cross.

But this should not strike us as odd. If things are as bad as I believe they are, and as many others insist they are, why should it surprise us if, at least for a time, success and numbers are against us? (Even if we do have great numbers and much blessing, we still do not measure success the way the world does.) Why should it surprise us that we must swim against the tide?

Professor John Howard Yoder, in his disquieting book *The Politics of Jesus,* outlines the Lord's strategy as recorded in Luke:

> After the move to Capernaum ([Luke] 4:31), Luke reports a rising tide of effectiveness among the multitudes, the sick, and the tax-gatherers. Soon the backlash of the religious establishment begins, with objections to Jesus' authority to forgive (5:21) and his disreputable associates (5:30). Almost immediately the opposition mounts to the point of angry scheming (6:11). Luke emphasizes that it was "in these days" that Jesus, after a night-long vigil, named twelve key messengers, first-fruits of a restored Israel. To organized opposition he responds with the formal founding of a new social reality. New teachings are no threat, as long as the teacher stands alone; a movement, extending his personality in both time and space, presenting an alternative to the structures that were there before, challenges the system as no mere words ever could.[13]

Yes, it is a movement that "challenges the system as no mere words ever could," and once again, in our day, Jesus beckons us to join His worldwide movement. He invites us to advance His Father's Kingdom, to become His disciples in word and deed, to be His friends and co-workers, laboring with Him to build His holy congregation, joining Him in His efforts to overthrow the forces of hell.

The prospects are grand, the potential more than words can express, the price costly beyond description. Who will follow this divine Way? Who will enlist in this sacred cause? The adventure of a lifetime is here for the taking, and this whole generation, from the youngest to the oldest, can be part of the pioneer mission.

It is time for revolution in the Church. Can we count you in?

# Notes

## Chapter 1: *A Dog Food Revolution?*

1. http://www.peteducation.com/pharmacy/revolution_selame.htm. There is even a promotional Revolution pen!

2. For the last few concepts, cf. Gordon Dryden and Jeannette Vos, *The Learning Revolution*, rev. and updated edition, Jonathan Mooney and David Cole, *Learning Outside the Lines: Two Ivy League Students with Learning Disabilities and ADHD Give You the Tools for Academic Success and Educational Revolution* (New York: Simon & Schuster, 2000); Madelyn Cain, *The Childless Revolution* (Cambridge, Mass.: Perseus, 2001). Also noteworthy are the recent spate of books written on the American Revolution (or its leaders, in particular), although I have never tracked such writings through the years and cannot really say if this represents an increase.

3. Snowboarders, skiers, skaters and surfers will certainly be interested in another groundbreaking product that is so pioneering it can only be called "The Revolution." What is it?

> The Revolution is a challenging training tool to improve balance and coordination skills for all sports. The board is also a fun way for snowboarders, skateboarders and surfers to practice and improve on techniques and stunts. The Revolution's patented design consists of a maple deck with molded undercarriage and independent polymer wheels that include shielded radial bearings.

Truly, as the Internet ad states, "THIS IS THE NEW REVOLUTION." More practical is the new "HydroMaid," a "water-powered garbage disposal [that] is revolutionary—an exciting new product for a promising new millennium." So the millennial revolution has even reached the garbage disposal industry!

4. http://supportservices.msn.com/us/netarticles.asp?iconimgkey=ns& titleimgkey=netsavvy&keywordkey=nsshop&contentPg=content/Net-Savvy/netsavvy_shopping.htm, June 27, 2001. The Internet provider Net Zero ran a "Join the revolution" promotion in 2001, echoing the words of Radio-

Shack. Not only does everyone seem to have a revolution these days, but everyone is inviting you to join as well!

5. Boston, Ma.: Harvard Business School, 2000. Notable also were Paul Hawken (et al.), *Natural Capitalism: Creating the Next Industrial Revolution* (Boston, Ma.: Back Bay, 2000); and—with a very striking title considering the subject matter—Reji Asakura's *Revolutionaries at Sony: The Making of the Sony PlayStation and the Visionaries Who Conquered the World of Video Games* (New York: McGraw-Hill, 2000). World conquerors indeed! In 1999 I believe the best-selling "revolution" books were devoted to the subject of new diets. See my *Revolution! The Call to Holy War* (Ventura, Calif.: Gospel Light, 2000), 49, 313, n. 23, for references. In 2001 many other books joined the "revolution" genre, including Patricia Seybold's *The Customer Revolution* (calling for innovations in customer relations, somehow dubbed a revolution (New York: Crown, 2001) and Steven Levy's *Hackers: Heroes of the Computer Revolution,* updated ed. (New York: Penguin, 2001); see also, e.g., Arthur Skulley, *B2B Exchanges: The Killer Application in the Business-To-Business Internet Revolution* (San Francisco: Harperbusiness, 2001); David S. Evans and Richard Schmalansee, *Paying with Plastic: The Digital Revolution in Buying and Borrowing* (Cambridge, Ma.: MIT Press, 2001); Robert Eccles and others, *The ValueReporting Revolution: Moving Beyond the Earnings Game* (New York: Wiley & Sons, 2001). Also worth mentioning is *Revolution: The Magazine for Digital Marketing* (see www.revolutionmagazine.com). The Sept. 4, 2001, issue of *PC* magazine was dubbed a "Special Collector's Issue," its subject, emblazoned in red and black letters, being "The 2nd PC Revolution." The headline of the September 2001 Special Double Issue of *Business 2.0* was, "Shhhhhhh! The Revolution Lives . . . Pass It On."

6. Leonard Sweet, *Post-Modern Pilgrims: First Century Passion for a 21st Century World* (Nashville: Broadman & Holman, 2000), xiv, citing the Roper Starch Worldwide Survey, "2004: A Personal Odyssey," Fast Company, September 1999, 262. www.fast-company.com/online/27/survey.html.

7. For a representative sampling, see Jim W. Goll, *The Coming Prophetic Revolution: A Call for Passionate, Consecrated Warriors* (Grand Rapids: Chosen, 2001); Darryl Scott and Steve Rabey, *Chain Reaction: A Call for Compassionate Revolution* (Nashville: Nelson, 2001); Sven E. Erlandson, *Spiritual But Not Religious: A Call to Religious Revolution in America* (San Jose: Writer's Showcase, 2000).

8. The songs are so numerous and widespread that I am unable to keep track of them. For the lyrics to three recent songs, see Brown, *Revolution!* 11, 282–83. The revolution theme colors everything we do at FIRE School of Ministry, since by definition we are "A Training Center for the Jesus Revolution." Our school's first CD, "By Life or By Death: Songs of the Revolution from FIRE School of Ministry," released in 2001, contains Charles Ciepiel's "Revolution Now" song, the lyrics of which were cited in *Revolution!* 11.

9. This was the primary message of *Revolution!* More concisely, see my shorter statement, "The Jesus Manifesto: A Call to Revolution," available for

free download and distribution on our ministry website, www.icnmin-istries.org, or from our school website, www.fire-school.org.

10. Hannah Arendt, *On Revolution* (repr., New York: Penguin, 1990), 27.

11. London: Orion Business Books, 1998. Many thanks to my dear British friend Derek Brown for making me aware of this book and giving me his own copy (to keep!).

12. Ibid., vii–viii, emphasis his.

13. See Arthur "Aaron" Katz, *Apostolic Foundations: The Challenge of Living an Authentic Christian Life* (Laporte, Minn.: Burning Bush, 1999). Apostolic church-planter John G. Lake (1870–1935) said, "I am interested in what constitutes the character of an apostle. The modern conception of an apostle is usually that he is a big church boss, but that was not the conception Jesus left. He took the twelve aside just before His departure, took a basin in His hand, tied a towel around His waist, knelt down and washed the feet of the lot of them, and when He finished He said to them, 'If I then, your Lord and Master, have washed your feet, ye also ought to wash one another's feet.' An apostle was not to be a big boss; he was to be like his Lord—a servant of all." See *The New John G. Lake Sermons* (Dallas: CFNI, reprint 1997), 2. My appreciation goes to Bryan Purtle, a School of Ministry graduate, for this reference.

### Chapter 2: *It's Time to Wake Up!*

1. Roger Kimball, *The Long March: How the Cultural Revolution of the 1960s Changed America* (San Francisco: Encounter, 2000), 5. Note that some of the material cited by Kimball to illustrate his points, especially from the pens of Norman Mailer and Allen Ginsberg, is quite explicit and offensive.

2. *How We Got Here: The 1970s: The Decade That Brought You Modern Life (For Better or Worse)* (New York: Basic, 2000), cited in ibid., 5.

3. "A Life of Learning," *The American Scholar*, summer 1991, 348, cited in ibid., 5–6.

4. *Slouching Towards Gomorrah: Modern Liberalism and American Decline* (New York: Regan, 1996), cited in Kimball, *The Long March*, 14. This is just a selection from Kimball.

5. I was informed by German Christian leaders in September 2000 that the current German government, part of the "1968 generation," is the first post-war government to refuse to say, "With the help of God," when taking the oath of office. Interestingly, at the end of 2001, a CNN news commentator stated that 2001 was the worst year in memory—with the possible exception of 1968. How telling!

6. "Mexican Student Movement," in Martin van Creveld, ed., *The Encyclopedia of Revolutions and Revolutionaries: From Anarchism to Zhou Enlai* (Jerusalem: Facts on File, 1996), 292.

7. George Leonard, "The End of Sex," *Esquire*, December 1982, 70, cited in Randy C. Alcorn, *Christians in the Wake of the Sexual Revolution: Recovering Our Sexual Sanity* (Portland, Ore.: Multnomah, 1985), 51.

8. Alcorn, *Christians in the Wake of the Sexual Revolution*, 51.

9. Ideologically speaking, this would be especially true of the liberal Church, since its leaders actually endorsed some aspects of the sexual revolution, as noted by Alcorn, *Christians in the Wake of the Sexual Revolution*, 51.

10. Very revealing of the times—but somewhat off the current subject—was the following mock ad: "Melvin, you've got to come home! We understand why you dropped out of our hypocritical conformist existence devoted to the acquisition of material things, to tune in on the peace, brotherhood and psychedelic joys of the turned-on Hippie Movement. It's just that we can no longer afford to send you the money you need to stay there. Mother and Dad."

11. Based on the saying of Leonard Ravenhill, "The opportunity of a lifetime must be seized during the lifetime of the opportunity," popularized by Steve Hill, the evangelist of the Brownsville Revival (1995–2000).

12. I have no doubt that these events were momentous; it is clear, however, that they did not signal the immediate end of the age, since we are still here, 45 years later and counting. Moreover, as I understand the Scriptures, Israel's return to the land and Jerusalem's return to Jewish control are signs of imminent spiritual revival in the midst of worldwide upheaval and shaking, rather than primarily being indicators of coming spiritual declension. See further, Michael L. Brown, *Our Hands Are Stained with Blood* (Shippensburg, Pa.: Destiny Image, 1992), esp. 99–106, 143–73.

13. Phil Enlow, Midnight Cry Ministries, http://www.midcry.org/revolution.htm.

14. Cf. Michael L. Brown, *The Revival Answer Book: Rightly Discerning the Contemporary Revival Movements* (Ventura, Calif.: Renew, 2001), 243–61; see also ibid., 163–77.

15. Two of our FIRE missionaries in Ivory Coast, Africa, Mark and Kim Butler, both in their forties, heard me read these book review excerpts in a message I preached in August 2001. Their response, received in an e-mail dated Dec. 4, 2001, is wonderful: "As we were thinking back on why we are here, it suddenly dawned on us that it is all because 'we have no discernment and are just youngsters following a Pied Piper into his fantasy.' Voila! We realized that, Yes!!! This is exactly why we left the comfort of home and family and friends and came over here to live in a dirty, smelly, disease-infested, hot, backbreaking land where even the people you try to help don't really appreciate it anyway. It is all because we are following a Pied Piper and his fantasy! It's all crystal clear now. We just wanted to send you some encouragement from deepest, darkest Africa. We constantly get tons of resistance, so we know that we're on the right trail. Every day is a challenge, but our God is bigger!!! After all, He is the God of all flesh; is there anything too hard for Him?! (Jer. 32:27)."

16. This reader/reviewer is not identified. I have no argument with the emphasis on God's coming wrath, a subject I have often emphasized in preaching and teaching over the course of many years (although surely in an inadequate way); see Michael L. Brown, *It's Time to Rock the Boat* (Shippensburg, Pa.: Destiny Image, 1993), 91–108; *How Saved Are We?* (Shippensburg, Pa.: Destiny Image, 1991), 51–57; as well as the following preached messages: "The Wrath of God" (audio only) and "Whatever Happened to the

Wrath of God?" (audio and video), available on our website (www.icnmin-istries.org). The audio messages can be downloaded without charge. I believe we are already experiencing the pangs of divine judgment, and I expect such judgments to increase and intensify until the end of the age. But God's judgment on the wicked means salvation for the righteous (see, for example, Psalm 98), and God's activity on the earth in this hour is hardly limited to judgment and wrath. Far from it!

17. http://gaytoday.badpuppy.com/adinfo.htm. My appreciation to Katie George and Kim Stephen, FIRE staff and School of Ministry grads, for finding this article on the Net.

18. Ibid.

19. Ibid.

20. Both Bill Bright, *Revolution Now!* (San Bernardino, Calif.: Campus Crusade, 1969), and Tom Skinner, *Words of Revolution: A Call to Involvement in the REAL Revolution* (Grand Rapids: Zondervan, 1970), had a chapter titled "The Greatest Revolutionary Ever."

21. William Ward Ayer, "Preaching to Combat the Present Revolution," *Bibliotheca Sacra* 124 (July 1967), 206–17, is representative of those who rightly, even passionately, diagnosed the radical problems of the day, but failed to present a radical solution, emphasizing rather a return to evangelical fundamentals. He stated, for example, that "preaching to combat the present revolution must involve a thorough pulpit indoctrination of the fundamentals of the Christian faith" (211), noting that, "Above all, the man in the pulpit who realistically faces our continuing, unprecedented revolution must preach evangelistically" (213). Obviously these statements are true in themselves but reflect a traditional response—"pulpit indoctrination . . . the man in the pulpit"—to an untraditional problem. More radical and comprehensive proposals, such as those advocated by Skinner, *Words of Revolution,* were hardly heeded.

22. You can read my testimony tract, "From LSD to Ph.D.," on our ICN Ministries website (readers might find my pre-saved "Drug Bear" picture, posted there, of interest!).

23. I was saved in such a church in 1971, part of the Italian Pentecostal denomination called the CCNA (Christian Church of North America).

24. Bram Eisenthal, "Canadian School Comes Under Fire for Revolutionary Student Handbook," *Jewish Telegraph Agency,* http://www.jta.org/story.asp?story=8746.

## Chapter 3: *The Church Is Not a Building*

1. William A. Beckham, *The Second Reformation: Reshaping the Church for the Twenty-First Century* (Houston: Touch Publications, 1995), 18, emphasis his.

2. The 50th of Luther's 95 Theses stated: "Christians are to be taught that if the pope knew the exactions of the indulgence preachers, he would rather that the basilica of St. Peter were burned to ashes than built up with the skin, flesh, and bones of his sheep."

3. Watchman Nee, *The Normal Christian Church Life* (Anaheim: Living Stream Ministry, 1980), emphasis his.

4. Johannes P. Louw and Eugene A. Nida, eds., *Greek-English Lexicon of the New Testament Based on Semantic Domains* (New York: United Bible Societies, 1988), vol. 1, 11.32 (henceforth cited as Louw-Nida).

5. *Yoke of Christ* (New York: Harper and Brothers, 1958), 113 (cited in Beckham, *Second Reformation*, 69).

6. Louw-Nida define *Church* simply as "the totality of congregations of Christians."

7. Beckham, *Second Reformation*, 42–43.

8. Nee, *The Normal Christian Church Life*, 169. His statement that "it is Judaism, not Christianity, which teaches that there must be sanctified places for divine worship" (ibid.) oversimplifies the Jewish position. Nee is correct, however, in his emphasis regarding Christianity. For thoughts on the terms *Judaism* and *Christianity*, see below, chapter 10. According to Frank A. Viola, *Rethinking the Wineskins*, rev. ed. (Brandon, Fla.: Present Testimony Ministry, 1998), 49, "What did the early church do when it grew too large to assemble in a single house? It did not erect a building, but simply multiplied and met in several other homes following the 'house to house principle' (Acts 2:46; 20:20). In this regard, New Testament scholarship today agrees that the early Church was essentially a network of home-based meetings. Hence if there is such a thing as a normal church, it is the church that meets in the house." Some of these verses, of course, mention the larger, public meeting together of the believers as well (e.g., Acts 2:46), and this seems to me to be the ideal model (as stressed by Beckham and many others): large, corporate meetings held on a regular basis, with the nucleus of Church life being expressed in small house meetings.

9. Nee, *The Normal Christian Church Life*, 169–70.

10. Louw-Nida, 42–43.

## Chapter 4: *The Body Is Not an Audience*

1. This, of course, was the goal of the Sinai Covenant, as stated in Exodus 19:5–6, a goal not realized through Israel's failure, representative of humanity's failure as a whole. On a certain level, the synagogue movement in general and Pharisaical Judaism in particular sought to elevate the spirituality of all Jews, the latter calling on all the people of Israel to live in priestly purity.

2. Professor Hendrik Kraemer, a scholar in world religions, notes how "extremely little the place of the laity was developed in the thinking of the Church between the 2nd and 16th centuries along . . . the 'hierarchical-ecclesiastical' line." See *A Theology of the Laity* (Philadelphia: Westminster, 1958), 71.

3. It should also be pointed out that the priests themselves were often biblically illiterate, as observed by a disciple of John Wycliffe, as noted by Benson Bobrick: "In Wycliffe's day . . . it was thought sufficient if the priest knew the Ten Commandments, the Paternoster (Our Father), the Creed and Ave (Hail Mary), 'with common parts of the Holy Writ.' " See *Wide As the Waters:*

*The Story of the English Bible and the Revolution It Inspired* (New York: Simon & Schuster, 2001), 49.

4. According to Kraemer, "The fundamental ideas of the Reformation promised to inaugurate a radical change in the whole conception and place of the laity. Luther, at a decisive moment, rejected obedience to the Church as embodied in the hierarchical authority of the Pope, in the name of obedience to the Word of God. Luther's conception of the Church, especially in his earlier, militant writings, was a frontal attack on the hierarchical conception of the Church. The idea of the clergy as such was rejected. In principle the distinction of 'clergy' and 'laity' fell away. . . . For the sake of order alone certain people are set apart by the congregation, 'ministers' who were not priests in the cultural sense, mediators between God and the congregation of God and man, but 'ministers of the Word' (*verbi divini* ministry). But in principle all that was contained in the newly conceived ministry (to teach and preach, to baptize, to administer Holy Communion, to bind and loose sins, to make intercession, to judge about doctrine and discern the spirits) belonged of right to every baptized Christian" (*A Theology of the Laity*, 61–62).

5. The literal meaning of the New Testament term *saints* is "holy ones."

6. Jesus as High Priest and Melchizedek the priest occur only in Hebrews. Acts 6:7 ("a large number of priests became obedient to the faith") simply states that a large number of Temple priests became believers in Yeshua.

7. See also Romans 15:16, where Paul makes reference to his "priestly duty of proclaiming the gospel of God, so that the Gentiles might become an offering acceptable to God, sanctified by the Holy Spirit."

8. For more on this, see below, chapter 6.

9. I thank God from the heart for every servant whom the Lord has placed on television to do His work, and I appreciate all those who are sincere and not mercenaries or self-promoters. (It is God's job more than ours to decide who is sincere and who is not.) On the other hand, I believe the Lord is not pleased with those who ask viewers or listeners to send in their prayer requests primarily as a means to gaining finances and growing a mailing list. How can this be right?

10. For thoughts on why the elders were called to pray for the sick in James 5:14–15, see Peter H. Davids, *The Epistle of James*, NIGTC (Grand Rapids: Eerdmans, 1982), 192–95.

11. Edwin Hatch, *The Organization of the Early Christian Churches* (New York: Longmans, Green and Co., 1901), 121–22.

12. By "membership," Hatch does not mean the formal church membership that is common today, but rather being a genuine part of the Body.

13. Hatch, *The Organization of the Early Christian Churches*, 121–22.

14. Ibid., 122.

15. Hence the requirements for leaders laid out in detail in 1 Timothy 3 and Titus 1 (see also 1 Peter 5:1–3; Hebrews 13:7); see also James 3:1: "Not many of you should presume to be teachers, my brothers, because you know that we who teach will be judged more strictly."

16. Part of thesis 8, "Out of the hands of bureaucratic clergy and on towards the priesthood of all believers," in his *Fifteen Theses toward the Re-Incarnation of Church;* see his *Houses That Change the World: The Return of the House Churches* (Waynesboro, Ga.: OM Publishing, 1998), xix (for all the theses, see xv–xxv). In a slightly abbreviated and differently worded form, these were first circulated on the Internet as "Fifteen Theses for a New Reformation."

17. This, of course, is the opposite of my point. The emphasis should be on inward spirituality, not outward appearance.

18. John Wesley, letter to Francis Asbury, with reference also to Thomas Coke, both of whom he had ordained and sent to America.

19. In many church circles, bishop refers simply to a pastoral leader, often with responsibility to shepherd other pastors or leaders, and it is based on the King James translation of 1 Timothy 3:1. In that sense it is a biblical term and is understandably used as such. I have often wondered, however, what would drive a leader to keep taking on new titles, as if the previous title/s of honor no longer sufficed.

20. Frank A. Viola, *Who Is Your Covering? A Fresh Look at Leadership, Authority, and Accountability,* 3rd, rev. ed. (Brandon, Fla.: Present Testimony Ministry, 1998), 26–27. He notes further that "Paul charges and implores 'the brethren' over thirty times in his first epistle to Corinth, and he writes as if no officers exist. . . . At the end of the book, Paul does tell the Corinthians to subject themselves to the self-giving Stephanas and his household. However, he potentially widens this group to others saying, 'and to everyone who does likewise.' Further, in the previous fifteen chapters, Paul instructs the whole church how to handle its own problems" (ibid., 27). With regard to Philippians 1:1, he comments, "While Paul does mention the overseers once in one of his letters, he does so in a very fleeting way—after he greets the church itself" (ibid.).

21. Ibid., 29.

22. Viola's list was not intended to be exhaustive.

23. If I were trying to make this a more precise analogy, I would say that the coach of the team was actually a player-coach, and that Jesus was the team's owner and CEO.

## Chapter 5: *Cult-Like or Cutting-Edge?*

1. *Swami* is used in several Indian languages for "master."

2. The fact that Jesus sent His disciples out was unique for the typical teacher-disciple relationship of the day.

3. For more discussion on the meaning of the cross, see Brown, *Revolution!* 218–43.

4. D. Müller, "Disciple," in Colin Brown, ed., *The New International Dictionary of New Testament Theology* (Grand Rapids: Zondervan, 1986), 2:362–67, 1:488.

5. This is one of the distinctives of Jesus' ministry: In the ancient world students would choose their teachers. Here the Teacher chooses His students! As

Müller wrote, "Whereas in [rabbinic] circles and in [Greek] philosophical schools a man made a voluntary decision to join the 'school' of his master and so become a disciple, with Jesus it was his call that was decisive (Lk. 5:1–11; cf. Matt. 5:18ff.). Jesus seized the initiative and called men into discipleship . . ." (ibid.).

6. Ibid., 1:488–89. According to Müller, this is "important for understanding the discipleship of Jesus," adding, "According to Mk. 1:17 and Lk. 5:10, the disciples are to be fishers of men. This is a colloquial phrase, meaning that in view of the impending reign of God, the disciples are to catch men for the coming kingdom by preaching the gospel and working in the name of Jesus (cf. Matt. 16:15ff.)."

7. Skinner, *Words of Revolution*, 55–56.

8. Skinner addressed this same question, responding: "This does not necessarily mean that God expects you to go out, take the last shirt off your back and live in abject poverty. It doesn't mean He plans for you to take everything you have, dump it, and live like a hermit. But it does mean that all that you are, and all that you have, is to be totally committed to Jesus Christ—that He owns you and everything you have—lock, stock and barrel. He has the right to do with you and all that you own as He pleases. That's the whole name of the game" (ibid., 56).

9. *Atlanta Journal-Constitution*, Sunday, Sept. 10, 2000, M1; the author of the article, John Blake, comments that "those who joined the [civil rights] movement still miss the adrenaline of being a part of something so monumental." My appreciation to Dennis and Colene Rouse, leaders of Victory Christian Center, Atlanta, for giving me this article.

10. According to New Testament theologian Hans Weder, "The self-understanding of Jesus, who saw the embodiment of the breaking in of the entirely new (the Kingdom of God) in his own person (cf. Luke 11:20 Q; 17:21), was reflected in the call which created the discipleship existence. This call is the indication of the nearness of God, who anticipates the human search for him and unexpectedly and uninvited enters the human life" ("Disciple, Discipleship," in David Noel Freedman, ed., *The Anchor Bible Dictionary* [New York: Doubleday, 1992], 2:208).

11. *Revolution Now!* 23–24.

12. For further thoughts on the principle of the revolutionary's dedication to a cause, see Brown, *Revolution!* 56–77.

13. Craig S. Keener notes that "the Essene sect at Qumran also described itself as 'the way'; this was a natural designation for a group that believed that it alone followed the way of righteousness." See his *IVP Bible Background Commentary: New Testament* (Downers Grove, Ill.: InterVarsity, 1993), on Acts 9:1–2.

14. This New Testament calling should be distinguished from the contemporary cult called the Way, founded by Victor Paul Weirwille.

## Chapter 6: *Revolutionary, Not "Rebelutionary"*

1. John Bevere rightly notes that this tendency is especially common among those in the Western world, stating, "My experience has been that

Westerners (dwellers of democratic nations of America and Europe) are some of the most resistant people to truly hearing the word of God. The reason is fundamental. It is hard to understand kingdom principles with a democratic mind-set." *Under Cover* (Nashville: Thomas Nelson, 2001), 9–10.

2. See Rodger Streitmatter, *Voices of Revolution: The Dissident Press in America* (New York: Columbia University, 2001), 202.

3. Michael L. Brown, *Whatever Happened to the Power of God?* (Shippensburg, Pa.: Destiny Image, 1991), 179.

4. I am aware that the slogan of the American Revolution was "Rebellion Against Tyrants Is Obedience to God," but I would still argue that the greater force driving the revolution was the cry for liberty rather than a call to rebellion in and of itself. Rather, the rebellion was a protest against oppression and injustice. In any event, the key is the last part of the phrase: "Obedience to God"—that must always be the dominant factor.

5. Don't panic and say to yourself, "Forty years! I can't wait forty years before God uses me!" Fear not. God was preparing Moses for a pretty big task, and he didn't have a worldwide body of believers to support him and work with him. Let's hope that your preparation—and mine—for full usefulness will not take forty years in the desert.

6. Watchman Nee, *Spiritual Authority* (New York: Christian Fellowship, 1972), 107–8. It was David Ravenhill who pointed out this section to me. One reason I cite Nee here is because his *Spiritual Authority* is often used to back up leadership authority that at times can be abusive—hence the value of this important, balancing statement from Nee. According to Frank Viola, *Who Is Your Covering?*, 104, Nee's book is "one of the most abused pieces of literature ever to be written in this century. Virtually every recent authoritarian movement has gotten mileage out of this book to support the power of heavy-handed leadership. While the book does contain some precious insights, its weaknesses render it dangerous in the wrong hands. Regrettably, Nee's book blurs the distinction between the Old and New Testament concept of authority and fails to distinguish between the way it works among dignitaries versus the church. In Nee's defense [and note that Viola has nothing but praise for a number of Nee's other writings], this book was never intended for a general audience. It is merely a transcription of messages that he gave to his apostolic co-workers in China."

7. Nee, *Spiritual Authority*, 108.

8. Although the NIV begins 1 Peter 3:1 with the words, "Wives, in the same way be submissive to your husbands," in a context that immediately follows Peter's teaching on the submission of slaves to their masters, the Greek word *homoios* can also be rendered "likewise" (cf. KJV) or "so, too." In any case, the comments of Edwin A. Blum on 1 Peter 3:1 (*Expositor's Bible Commentary*, 12:236) are certainly accurate and summarize the point I am trying to make: "'In the same way' *(homoios)* in both v. 1 and v. 7 points back to 2:13. Christian wives are not to be in subjection like slaves but rather the principle of Christian subjection to God's will relates to every class and every situation."

9. For more on this, see chapter 7.

10. Nee, *Spiritual Authority,* 108–9.

11. Ibid., 109. For slightly different translations of these same passages, cf. Watchman Nee, *Authority and Submission* (Anaheim: Living Stream Ministry, 1993).

12. See Edgar Snow, "Revolution in China in Mao Tse-Tung, Genesis of a Communist: Childhood," in James Chowning Davies, ed., *When Men Revolt and Why,* 2nd ed. (New Brunswick, N.J.: Transaction, 1997), 68.

13. Cited in Thomas Merton, ed., *Gandhi on Non-Violence: Selected Texts from Mohandas K. Gandhi's Non-Violence in Peace and War* (New York: New Directions, 1964), 28.

14. D. A. Carson, *Expositor's Bible Commentary,* 8:133, on Matthew 5:5.

15. *Matthew Henry's Commentary on the Bible* (from the Sage Digital Library CD-ROM, Albany, Ore.: Sage Software), on Matthew 5:5.

16. Peter Ackerman and Jack DuVall, *A Force More Powerful: A Century of Nonviolent Conflict* (New York: St. Martin's, 2000), 1. The words in brackets were supplied from information on the six-part, two-video documentary of the same name, a moving documentary that I highly recommend. My only real caveat with the book itself, which is quite enlightening, is its surprising and unjustifiable inclusion of the Palestinian Intifada, even in its nonviolent forms, since the Intifada, above all, was violent and bloody, at times engaging in terrorism and virtually always fueling the fires of anti-Semitism.

17. Gordon Lindsay, *John Alexander Dowie: A Life Story of Tragedies, Trials and Triumphs* (Dallas: Christ for the Nations, 1980), 274.

## Chapter 7: *Covering or Smothering?*

1. At the end of the next chapter we will address the concept of "the pastor and his board." For now let's just go along with the illustration without questioning whether such a concept is biblical.

2. The context of Psalm 105:15 has to do with God warning the heathen nations not to touch the patriarchs—Abraham, Isaac and Jacob. If it is applied to us today, it should be applied as a warning to the world not to touch God's people, all of whom are the Lord's anointed. One could even argue that this verse can be used as a warning to abusive leaders: Don't touch God's anointed—meaning His sheep!

3. According to New Testament scholar William L. Lane, the Greek verb rendered "obey" in Hebrews 13:17 "certainly demands obedience. But the specific quality of the obedience which *peithesthai* asks is not primarily derived from a respect for constituted structures of authority. It is rather the obedience that is won through persuasive conversation that follows from it. . . . The writer carries his injunction a step further with the second verb *hueikein,* 'to submit to someone's authority.' . . . The community is summoned to respect the authority with which the leadership has been invested by God" (*Hebrews 9–13, Word Biblical Commentary* [Dallas: Word, 1991], 554). See also Viola, *Who Is Your Covering?,* 35–36.

4. At the risk of belaboring this point, I make reference once again to chapter 6 of this book.

5. The pastor could also point to the Scriptures for both of these examples, stating that there were arranged marriages in the Bible and that God commands husband and wife to be fruitful and multiply!

6. I want to emphasize again how important it is to honor authority, but not in a mindless, irresponsible way. To give a personal example, as a new believer I had no desire to go to college—an unconscious carryover from my counterculture, anti-establishment mentality. But it was very important to my parents that I go, and when my father lovingly challenged me by the Scriptures—holding me to what I believed and asking me how I could reconcile my choice not to attend college with the strong request of my mother and father that I go—I agreed on the spot to change my plans and seek to enroll. This was a good case of the blessing that comes from honoring and obeying parents and other authority figures (indeed, my education has played an important part in my overall calling). But note: God did not speak to me not to go, and I was not violating my conscience by going to school. I had no legitimate, scriptural reason, therefore, to refuse my father's request.

7. This is the explicit position of Bevere, *Under Cover*, 135: "The only time—and I want to emphasize the only exception in which we are not to obey authorities—is when they tell us to do something that directly contradicts what God has stated in His Word. In other words, we are released from obedience when leaders tell us to sin. However, even in those cases we are to keep a humble and submitted attitude." A commonly taught variation of this is: "You do what your authorities tell you to do unless it is immoral, unethical or unscriptural." Both of these positions, however, fail to address issues of conscience or the clear directives of the Holy Spirit, although Bevere goes as far as to state, "It doesn't matter what you believe you've heard in prayer; you are rebelling against God's authority if it goes against the directives of authorities in your life!" (ibid., 159). Such statements do not factor in verses such as Romans 14:23, which teaches that whatever is not done in faith is sin. If a leader tells a congregant, therefore, to do something that violates his or her conscience and cannot be done in faith, that leader is actually telling the congregant to sin. Also, doesn't the Word itself teach us that there are certain times when we must obey God rather than man? If a leader tells a believer to disregard what the Spirit has spoken to him and submit to the leader's directives, that leader is telling the believer to disobey the Word. I recognize that *Under Cover* is addressing the terrible problem of lawlessness in the Body today, and for this John Bevere is to be commended. But this does not mean that some of the positions he takes in the book do not need to be modified and/or qualified.

8. 1 Corinthians 7:21. Bevere, *Under Cover*, devotes a whole chapter to the subject of "Unfair Treatment," 160–77, making this excellent closing comment: "Spiritual authority is promised to those who suffer like Christ. The greater hardship you endure, the greater the authority God entrusts to you. Again, you see that God sets you up for a blessing when you encounter unrea-

sonable authority. But will you respond correctly and receive the blessing, or will you become resentful and bitter? The choice is yours. Choose the way of the overcomer, which is life!" Note, however, that he specifically cites 1 Peter 2:13, 18 to call believers to submit to harsh and cruel authorities of every kind, just as slaves must submit to harsh and cruel masters. Quite explicitly in the context of *Under Cover,* therefore, this means that believers should submit in just the same way to harsh and cruel pastors and spiritual leaders. As we have emphasized, this is *not* the teaching of Scripture.

9. See above, chapter 6.

10. Peter H. Davids, *The Book of First Peter,* NICNT (Grand Rapids: Eerdmans, 1990), 180.

11. Tom Marshall, *Understanding Leadership* (Lynnwood, Wash.: Emerald WA, 1992), 111. I am indebted to David Ravenhill for this selection.

12. Ibid.

13. Theoretically one could argue that if God spoke to the evangelist, perhaps through an audible voice, and commanded him to give an altar call, then he should obey God and not man, suffering the consequences. But I have yet to encounter such a situation in more than two decades of itinerant ministry.

14. Ibid., 110.

15. Viola asks, "If the Bible is silent with respect to the idea of 'covering,' what do people mean when they ask, 'Who is your covering?' Most people (if pressed) would rephrase the question as: 'To what person are you accountable?' But this raises another sticky point: the Bible never consigns accountability to human beings. It consigns it exclusively to God (Matt. 12:36; 18:23; Luke 16:2; Rom. 3:19; 14:12; 1 Cor. 4:5; Heb. 4:13; 13:17; 1 Pet. 4:5)." *Who Is Your Covering?*, 14. Viola is quick to note that "there is a healthy form of accountability in the church," devoting discussion to that very subject later in his book.

16. Nee, *Spiritual Authority,* 116.

17. Ibid.

18. Ibid.

19. Ibid., 116–17.

20. Ibid., 117.

21. Ibid.

22. Viola states, "What Jesus is condemning in these passages is not oppressive leaders as such, but the hierarchical form of leadership that dominates the Gentile world. . . . What is the hierarchical form of leadership? It is the leadership style that is rooted in the benighted idea that power and authority flow from the top down in a chain-of-command social structure. The hierarchical leadership style is based on a worldly concept of power. This explains why it is endemic to all traditional bureaucracies, from the vicious forms of liege-lord and master-slave relationships to the highly stylized and regulated spheres of modern military and corporate America." *Who Is Your Covering?*, 19.

23. Davids, *First Peter,* 180–81.

## Chapter 8: *Confronting the Pastoral Fraternity*

1. Cited in Lawrence Khong, *The Apostolic Cell Church: Practical Strategies for Growth and Outreach from the Story of Faith Community Baptist Church* (Singapore: Touch, 2000), 101. He comments: "No wonder studies rate the pastorate as one of the most stressful occupations in the world!"

2. In my illustration I have a reason for saying that a denomination sent him to plant the work: I want to avoid yet another "ministerial labor union" objection, "By what authority are you doing this?" That question is the subject of the next chapter.

3. One of the better books on this subject is by Francis Frangipane, *The House of the Lord* (Lake Mary, Fla.: Creation House, 1991). It should be noted, of course, that God will often raise up one senior leader among the other leaders of the church of the city, something that is frequently welcomed— or even strongly desired—by the others.

4. The territorial position is often supported by reference to the relationship between Saul and David. As the argument goes, "David (the associate or youth pastor) didn't try to steal the kingdom away from Saul (the senior pastor). Rather, he ran away as far as he could and refused to hurt the Lord's anointed. So when differences arise between a senior and junior leader, the junior leader should get out of town."

Obviously we should never try to harm or bring down leaders with whom we differ, even if God Himself has guaranteed their downfall (as was the case with Saul). But what in the world does this have to do with a difference between leaders? Is the local pastor the king of the entire region? Really, the Saul-David analogy has been overused—and in many ways misused.

Consider the following: (1) Any pastor using the Saul-David analogy to discourage someone from starting a "competing" work in the same city is thereby saying that he is a Saul. What leader would ever want to say that? (2) David was already anointed king and already knew that Saul's entire kingdom would soon be his. Are we to assume this part of the scenario, too? (3) David did not leave Saul's territory for ethical reasons but because he was fleeing for his life. Saul kept trying to murder him! (4) David received a prophetic word from God to *stay* in Israelite territory rather than flee outside of Israel's borders (1 Samuel 22:5). (5) David prayed for God to destroy his enemies, including Saul. Is this how we should pray today in a dispute with another pastor? (Check out Psalm 59 for a prime example of this.) (6) David did nothing to discourage people from gathering around him.

Wisdom and sound biblical interpretation caution us not to use the Saul-David analogy too quickly. You do not want to imply that you are a Saul, nor do you want to imply that you are the king of the region. God is jealous over His rightful reign.

5. Note also that the introductory verses in seven of Paul's epistles list other leaders alongside of him: 1 Corinthians 1:1 (Sosthenes); 2 Corinthians 1:1; Philippians 1:1; Colossians 1:1; Philemon 1 (all with Timothy); 1 Thessalonians 1:1; 2 Thessalonians 1:1 (both with Silas and Timothy). It is interesting to note that after Peter, Barnabas and Paul, and then James, give their

views on the Gentile question in Acts 15, all of them being in agreement, the letter sent to the Gentile believers then reads (in part), "It seemed good to the Holy Spirit and to us not to burden you with anything beyond the following requirements" (Acts 15:28). That is the ideal model!

6. Khong, *The Apostolic Cell Church*, 109.

7. Team ministry presents many challenges, of course, and as my colleague Dr. Josh Peters teaches our FIRE students, team ministry can succeed only when personal agendas are crucified and the leaders are not insecure. Otherwise team ministry will not realize its potential, and it may even fail. Also, team ministry must not quench individual gifting and calling but rather enhance it. A poem I wrote almost a decade ago called "Covenantal Crunch" reflects my frustration with an unhealthy team emphasis and articulates the concern of the group smothering the individual:

> Covenantal, covenantal, covenantal crunch,
> Judging, quenching, crowding, crushing—having you for lunch!
>
> "Confirmation, confirmation, confirmation, please!
> With our covenantal strictures you'll be in a squeeze!
>
> "Submit! Conform! Become like us! Soon you'll fit our mold.
> We'll cramp out your identity in our stranglehold.
>
> "You're much too independent; you think you hear God well.
> But if He has a word to speak, it's the group He'll tell!
>
> "We're playing by the rules we wrote; what we build will last.
> We have endless meetings; you just pray and fast!
>
> "You talk about anointing, of moving in the Lord.
> Well that stuff's not impressive. God's not on our board!"
>
> My brothers please do hear me. I've got a word for you:
> If the prophets were alive, them you'd shut up, too!
>
> Paul you'd call a rebel; John Huss, an arrogant man;
> Luther you'd brand unteachable. He wouldn't fit the plan!
>
> Whitefield would be cast out; William Booth misunderstood;
> "You're breaking with our pattern! It's not for the common good.
>
> "Come here under our covering. Please don't rock the boat"—
> But, no, I see those tentacles, reaching for my throat!
>
> Submission is a good word, authority a good thing—
> It brings men into freedom; but what do your codes bring?
>
> So here is my conclusion. This is what I've found:
> Maybe you are "bonding"—but I don't want to be bound!

8. This point was first made to me in 1993 by my dear Indian co-worker and friend P. Yesupadam.

9. Notice also the usage of *we* and *us* in Peter's other speeches in Acts (for example, 3:11–15, with John; 4:18–20, again with John; 5:29–32, Peter and the other apostles).

10. *Who Is Your Covering?*, 24.

11. See below, n. 13, for references in Scripture.

12. Unless, of course, it simply refers to a shepherd of sheep (as, for example, in Luke 2:8). My FIRE colleague Steve Alt points out that if you asked a Greek-speaking believer in the first century, "Who is your pastor?" his most natural response would be "Jesus!" He is called the Good Shepherd (Pastor!), the Great Shepherd (Pastor!) and the Chief Shepherd (Pastor!); see John 10:14; Hebrews 13:20; 1 Peter 5:4. On the other hand, every believer should be part of a regular gathering of believers (see, for example, Hebrews 10:25), and the New Testament presupposes that believers will also know who their leaders are (compare Hebrews 13:7, 17, 24). There is no biblical justification for independent, unattached Christians.

13. Apostle: Acts 14:14 (Barnabas); 1 Thessalonians 2:6 (Silas); Galatians 1:19 (James); Romans 16:7 (Andronicus and Junia); 1 Corinthians 15:7 (unnamed); cf. further Luke 11:49; 1 Corinthians 12:18; John 13:16; 2 Corinthians 8:23; Philippians 2:25; prophet: Acts 11:27; 13:1; 15:32, referring to Judas and Silas; 21:10; 1 Corinthians 12:28–29; 14:29, 32, 37; Ephesians 2:20; 3:5; evangelist: Acts 21:8, with reference to Philip, and 2 Timothy 4:5, where Timothy is exhorted to do the work of an evangelist; teacher: Acts 13:1, with prophets; 1 Corinthians 12:28–29, listed along with apostles and prophets—but with no mention of pastors; 1 Timothy 2:7; 2 Timothy 1:11, both times, Paul speaking about himself; 1 Timothy 1:7; 2 Timothy 4:3; 2 Peter 2:1, 3, negatively; Hebrews 5:12; James 3:1. My appreciation to Steve Alt for these references.

14. Remarkably, a response paper produced by a major Pentecostal denomination recently stated, "Prophets in the New Testament are never described as holding an officially recognized position as in the case with pastors and evangelists." But where does the New Testament ever mention pastors or evangelists "holding an officially recognized position," and where does it say that prophets (or apostles) did not? And what scriptural support is there for the statement that "there are, and ought to be, apostolic- and prophetic-type ministries in the Church, without individuals being identified as filling such an office"? Doubtless there are some spiritual abuses in the current apostle-prophet leadership movement rightly corrected in this paper, but its tone at times is surprising and even judgmental, stating, for example, "It is very tempting for persons with an independent spirit and an exaggerated estimate of their own importance in the kingdom of God to declare organization and administrative structure to be of human origin," and, "Structure set up to avoid a previous structure can soon become dictatorial, presumptuous, and carnal while claiming to be more biblical than the old one outside the new order or organization."

Cannot the same be said about the "previous structure" and its leaders? Why limit the criticism to the "new order"? See "Endtime Revival: Spirit-Led and Spirit-Controlled, A Response to Resolution 16," adopted by the Assemblies of God on Aug. 11, 2000, http://www.ag.org/top/beliefs/position_papers/0000_index.cfm.

15. If you are sent to a foreign country, then you are a missionary—but what does that mean? What kind of missionary? With what primary calling?

16. I understand, of course, that in America and many other countries, legal regulations require religious organizations to have governing boards in place. But the solution is simple: The leadership team is the board, and all of them should qualify as elders based on 1 Timothy and Titus 1.

## Chapter 9: *By What Authority Do You Do These Things?*

1. Leonard Ravenhill, *America Is Too Young to Die* (Minneapolis: Bethany, 1979), 24.

2. Philip Melanchthon, *The Life and Acts of Martin Luther* (originally published in Wittenberg, Germany, 1549; Albany, Ore.: AGES Software, 1997), 32.

3. According to Reformation scholar Roland H. Bainton, "Very naturally Luther was constantly asked, 'By what authority doest thou these things?' Bist du allein klug? Are you alone wise? His answer was that he acted by the authority of Holy Scripture." *The Reformation of the Sixteenth Century* (Boston: Beacon, 1952), 44, cited in Don Clasen, *Submission to Spiritual Authority: A Definitive Treatment of a Modern Day Controversy* (Lindale, Tex.: Irenicon, 1981), 55.

4. There will always be a faithful remnant, and if you are alone in your beliefs, it is a good indication that you are in error, since Jesus has a multi-membered Body on the earth today. So beware of the "I-alone-have-the-truth" mentality.

5. If you have never read the 95 Theses, you would be surprised at how deeply they reflect the existing system, as Luther constantly refers to the proper role of the Pope (without in the least rejecting that office); does not dispute the specific class of priests (as opposed to arguing clearly for the priesthood of every believer; rather he refers to "clergy" and "laity"); speaks of purgatory; makes reference to the mother of God (the classic Catholic description of Mary) as well as to venial sins and the Mass; and does not at all repudiate indulgences, per se, but rather their abuses (famously, in #27). This is eye-opening! Luther even wrote apologetically to the Pope, after his Theses received wide, unexpected circulation, saying, "It is a mystery to me how my theses . . . were spread to so many places. They were meant exclusively for our academic circle here [and written] in such a language [Latin] that the common people could hardly understand" (cited in Bobrick, *Wide As the Waters*, 87). It was only a few years later that Luther could speak of "the devil, Pope, bishops, tyrants, and heretics" in one breath (e.g., in his *Larger Catechism*, end of Third Petition).

6. These accusations, more often than not, are accompanied by references to the Saul-David or David-Absalom syndrome, with all parties involved fashioning themselves to be the David of the hour! Generally speaking, the much-loved book by Gene Edwards, *A Tale of Three Kings: A Study of Brokenness* (repr., Wheaton: Tyndale, 1992), is also read by people on both sides, each pointing to the other side as representing either Saul or Absalom. For further thoughts on this, see chapter 8, n. 4.

7. Bonamy Dobreé, *John Wesley* (New York: Macmillan, 1933; Albany, Ore.: AGES Software, 1997), 48–49.

8. "William & Catherine Booth," *Christian History* 26 (Carol Stream, Ill.: Christianity Today, 1997).

9. "Baptist Churches in U.S.A.," in Daniel G. Reid, ed., *Dictionary of Christianity in America* (Downers Grove, Ill.: InterVarsity, 1990; part of the Quick-Verse 7.0 Library).

10. R. D. Linder, "Williams, Roger (1603–1683)," in *Dictionary of Christianity in America.*

11. Ibid. Interestingly, Adoniram Judson, the leader of the first missionary team to sail from America overseas (leaving in 1812), was a Presbyterian whose entire support came from Presbyterian churches. But as he and his wife, Nancy, studied the Scriptures while sailing to India, they became convinced that believer baptism, rather than infant baptism, was biblically correct, and they were baptized by William Carey upon their arrival in India. This cost them all their support, but the Baptist churches were quick to pick them up.

12. Ibid.

13. Ibid.

14. "Roger Williams," in J. D. Douglas and Philip W. Comfort, eds., *Who's Who in Christian History* (Wheaton: Tyndale, 1992; part of the QuickVerse 7.0 Library).

15. http://ag.org/top/about/where.cfm.

16. http://www.ag.org/top/about/history.cfm. Edith Blumhofer, widely recognized as the leading historian of the Assemblies of God, gives this succinct account: "Formed in April 1914 in Hot Springs, Arkansas, the Assemblies of God (AG), with well over 15 million adherents, is today the largest Pentecostal denomination in the world. The denomination began inauspiciously when some 300 believers responded to a call to a convention at Hot Springs. Approximately 120 of them were delegates from scattered Pentecostal ministries who shared concerns about their movement's future. While they nurtured an intense dislike for established denominations, they concluded that limited cooperation would be in their best interests and created the General Council of the Assemblies of God. Refusing to adopt a statement of faith, they did agree to encourage support for foreign missions and Bible institute education and to issue credentials to would-be workers who met certain qualifications. They also stated their intention to disapprove theological and practical 'error.'

"... In 1918 the denomination excluded some who questioned its view of evidential tongues. The trend toward conformity was reinforced. In four years it had become evident that, rhetoric aside, the Assemblies of God was a denomination rather than the loosely structured fellowship it claimed to be. When it adopted a constitution in 1927, the formal process was complete" (E. L. Blumhofer, "Assemblies of God," in *Dictionary of Christianity in America*).

17. Ibid.

18. E. B. Batson, "Bunyan, John (1628–1688)," in *Who's Who in Christian History*.

19. "John Bunyan and the Pilgrim's Progress" *Christian History* 11 (Carol Stream, Ill.: Christianity Today, 1997).

20. When Whitefield informed John and Charles Wesley of his plan to preach outdoors, John Wesley was shocked, remarking, "It is a mad notion." Church biographer John Pollock notes that Whitefield's plan would have seemed "indecent, indecorous, almost certainly illegal because of the Conventicle Act except at a public hanging, where admittedly the Wesleys had [previously] addressed the crowds . . . ," adding that John Wesley's private conviction on the matter (which he did not share with Whitefield) was: "I should have thought the saving of souls almost a sin if it had not been in a church." See John Pollock, *George Whitefield and the Great Awakening* (Tring, Herts, England: Lion, 1972), 76–77.

21. Rev. Andrew Thompson, *The Life of Dr. Owen* (Albany, Ore.: AGES Software, 1997), 10.

22. Ibid., 10–11. Interestingly, Owen, too, had some blind spots, not recognizing that some of the "Judaical" (that is, Jewish) traditions he rejected may have been biblical and more ancient than some of the unquestioned practices of the Church. For more on this, see the next chapter. It is possible, however, that he was speaking of unbiblical Jewish practices, which should also be rejected.

### Chapter 10: *Have You Read the Epistle of Jacob Lately?*

1. The first and last paragraph are cited in James Carroll, *Constantine's Sword: The Church and the Jews: A History* (Boston: Houghton Mifflin, 2001), 213; the middle paragraph is excerpted from Brown, *Our Hands Are Stained with Blood*, 10; the quotation from the words of Jesus at the end of the last paragraph is from Luke 19:27.

2. See Brown, *Our Hands Are Stained with Blood*, 11.

3. Carroll, *Constantine's Sword*, 213.

4. Cited in Brown, *Our Hands Are Stained with Blood*, 11. Chrysostom preached on this topic because his congregants were showing an interest in Judaism. See J. N. D. Kelly, *Golden Mouth: The Story of John Chrysostom—Ascetic, Preacher, Bishop* (Grand Rapids: Baker, 1995), 63–66.

5. Edward H. Flannery, *The Anguish of the Jews: Twenty-three Centuries of Anti-Semitism* (New York/Mahwah, N.J.: Paulist, 1985), 1, cited in Brown, *Our Hands Are Stained with Blood*, xii.

6. According to Michael Hakeem, "The historian, Professor Friedrich Heer, is authority for the knowledge that Hitler 'was prepared to concede that Luther had prepared the way for his own work.' He quotes Hitler as saying, as early as 1918: 'He saw the Jew as we are only now beginning to see him today.'" http://www.ffrf.org/fttoday/back/hakeem/holocaust4.html. I would note that this article and the article of Jim Walker (see below, notes 14–15), both posted on the Internet, are critical of all religious beliefs, being posted on "no belief" or "infidel" websites. Nonetheless, their recitation of the facts of Luther's anti-Semitism and the Nazi use of his writings cannot be ignored, and I cite these articles because of their easy accessibility.

7. Before running to Luther's defense, claiming that he was old and sick when he wrote these things, remember your reaction to the "Kill the Niggers!" sermons. Luther also used vulgar, profane expressions in some of his other writings.

8. See *Our Hands Are Stained with Blood*, 192, note 30.

9. The most recent, one-volume edition was published in 1985 by Holmes and Meier.

10. For references, see Brown, *Our Hands Are Stained with Blood*, 89–97, 205–7, 238.

11. See Martin Luther, *Vom Schem Hamphoras (Concerning the Unutterable Name of the Lord)*, ed. and trans. by Gerhard Falk, *The Jew in Christian Theology* (Jefferson, N.C.: McFarland, 1992), 167.

12. See Brown, *Our Hands Are Stained with Blood*, 52, and 192, note 30.

13. Selected from Luther's *Concerning the Jews and Their Lies.*

14. Cited in the Internet article by Jim Walker, "Martin Luther's Dirty Little Book: On the Jews and Their Lies," http://www.nobeliefs.com/luther.htm.

15. Walker, "Martin Luther's Dirty Little Book."

16. For extensive bibliographical references, see Brown, *Our Hands Are Stained with Blood;* idem, *Answering Jewish Objections to Jesus, Volume One: General and Historical Objections* (Grand Rapids: Baker, 2000), 101–96. Some of the most recent, widely read studies include Carroll, *Constantine's Sword*, who relies especially on secondary sources, and David I. Kertzer, *The Popes Against the Jews: The Vatican's Role in the Rise of Modern Anti-Semitism* (New York: Knopf, 2001), working directly with recently released primary sources.

17. For references, see immediately above, note 16.

18. See Brown, *Our Hands Are Stained with Blood*, 117–53; in reviewing the important volume of Dan Cohn-Sherbok, *The Crucified Jew: Twenty Centuries of Christian Anti-Semitism* (originally published in London, by HarperCollins, 1992), in *The Journal of the Evangelical Theological Society* (1998), I wrote: "Can those who hold to the veracity of the New Testament witness and the fundamental correctness of a universal gospel mission demonstrate that 'Christian' anti-Semitism is a horrible aberration rather than a natural consequence of the foundational documents? In my judgment, this can only be done by repudiating supersessionism (i.e., replacement theology) as unbiblical, acknowledging the Church's forsaking of her Jewish roots, and reaffirming God's eternal purposes for the Jewish people (as reflected by their

return to the Land)." Of course, many fine Christians who hold to the belief that the Church has replaced Israel (replacement theologians) are not anti-Semites in any way. But this does not lessen the widespread view—which is also my conviction—that replacement theology was the major open door through which anti-Semitism infiltrated the Church.

19. By Jewish roots, I do not primarily mean rabbinic or traditional Jewish roots (except insofar as they reflect biblical truth), nor do I mean that we should have a superficial fascination with everything Jewish—which is often nothing more than a sentimental, soulish fascination that does not bear spiritual fruit.

20. Keener, *IVP Bible Background Commentary: New Testament*, 358–59, notes that "Roman citizens had three names. As a citizen, Saul had a Roman cognomen ('Paul,' meaning 'small'); his other Roman names remain unknown to us. As inscriptions show was common, his Roman name sounded similar to his Jewish name (Saul, from the name of the Old Testament's most famous Benjamite). This is not a name change; now that Paul is moving in a predominantly Roman environment, he begins to go by his Roman name, and some of Luke's readers recognize for the first time that Luke is writing about someone of whom they had already heard."

21. In the New Testament, the name of the patriarch Jacob is written as *Yakob* (without the case ending), while all other Jacobs are written as *Yakobus* (and misleadingly rendered as "James" in our English Bibles).

22. Spanish biblical translations render *Yakobus* with "Santiago." (I am not sure of the reason for this). Some readers might be interested to know that the English rendering of *Yakobus* with "James" was not influenced by King James and the King James Version, since that rendering predates the KJV.

23. By Hebrew/Aramaic background, I do not mean that the New Testament was originally written in Hebrew but rather that (1) almost all its authors were Jews whose first language would have been Aramaic or Hebrew; (2) some of the oral traditions, and perhaps some written sources underlying the New Testament, were communicated in Aramaic and/or Hebrew; (3) the authors were accustomed to Jewish/Semitic ways of thinking. For a critique of some dangerous trends that go too far in trying to recover the alleged Hebrew background, see Michael L. Brown, "Recovering the Inspired Text? An Assessment of the Work of the Jerusalem School in the Light of Understanding the Difficult Words of Jesus," *Mishkan* 17/18:38–64, available on our website, www.icnministries.org.

24. Note that the Greek word *synagoges* could be used for any kind of meeting or meeting place, be it a secular gathering or a religious gathering of any kind. In other words, in New Testament times it did not necessarily refer to a Jewish meeting place. This explains verses such as Acts 13:5: "When they arrived at Salamis, they proclaimed the word of God in the Jewish synagogues." Obviously, if all "synagogues/meeting places" were Jewish, such an expression would not be needed. See also Acts 14:1; 17:1; 17:10. According

to the Louw-Nida Lexicon, the word's basic meaning is "an assembled group of worshipers or members of such a group—'assembly, congregation.' "

25. In Acts 13:43 a number of translations do render *synagoges* with "congregation" (KJV; NIV) or the like, since the context virtually demands it. Other versions, however, still render it "synagogue"—for example, the NASB's "the meeting of the synagogue" (similarly, the NRSV).

26. Would a different image come to mind if these verses instead spoke of those "who claimed to be Jews but are not, but are an assembly of Satan"? Perhaps they were not even Jews at all! Although most commentators do not (understandably) see this interpretation as a possibility, it should at least be considered. David H. Stern, *Jewish New Testament Commentary* (Clarksville, Md.: Jewish New Testament Publications, 1992), 795–96, states that, "Yochanan [John] writes about Gentiles who call themselves Jews but aren't—on the contrary, they are a synagogue of Satan, the Adversary. . . . Perhaps they, like the Gentile Judaizers of the book of Galatians, adopted a smattering of Jewish practices and tried to force them on Jewish Christians." He interacts with the normal interpretation—namely, that these truly are Jews—but notes that "nowhere in the New Testament are unbelieving Jews called non-Jews," dealing with Romans 2:28–29 in this context as well.

27. Keener, *IVP Bible Background Commentary: New Testament*, 694.

28. Stern, *Jewish New Testament Commentary*, 728–29, states: "Ya'akov [Jacob/James] is talking neither about a Christian church service nor a gathering of Jewish nonbelievers but a Messianic synagogue. He would not refer to 'your synagogue' and assume his readers were in charge of seating visitors if the synagogue was not controlled by Messianic Jews" (729). As for 5:14, where *ekklesia* is used, Stern simply renders, "He should call for the elders of the congregation. . . ." So most of our English Bibles have it backwards, translating *synagogue* with "assembly" and *congregation* with "church"! What a difference two little words make.

29. Albert Barnes, on James 2:2; see *Barnes' Notes on the New Testament* (Electronic Edition STEP Files Copyright 1999, Parsons Technology).

30. William Tyndale rendered Matthew 16:18 with "I will build my congregation," consistently translating *ekklesia* with "congregation" (see, for example, his rendering of well-known passages in Ephesians 5, where "Christ is the head of the congregation"; "Christ loved the congregation, and gave himself for it, to sanctify it, and cleansed it in the fountain of water through the word, to make it unto himself, a glorious congregation without spot or wrinkle"). His traditional contemporaries hotly opposed this practice. See Bobrick, *Wide As the Waters*, 112–13, and note the opening quote to chapter 3 from Richard Bancroft, making it a translation rule for the King James Version that "the Word *Church* [was] not to be translated *Congregation*. . . ."

31. In this immediate scriptural context, many have pointed to Acts 1:6–8 as proof that Jesus was telling His (all Jewish) disciples that they were mistaken in thinking God was going to restore the kingdom to Israel. Rather, He was saying that the timing of that event, which they were quite right in expecting, was not their concern at that moment. Their concern was fulfill-

ing the Great Commission in the power of the Spirit. For a fair exegetical statement, not reading anything into the text either way, see F. F. Bruce, *The Book of Acts,* rev. ed., NICNT (Grand Rapids: Eerdmans, 1988), 35–36.

32. Notice that the first word Paul associated with the Kingdom of God in Romans 14:17 was "righteousness" (see also Matthew 6:33), hardly an abstract spiritual concept. Commenting on Acts 14:22, Richard N. Longenecker notes that Paul and Barnabas encouraged the believers "to remain in the faith, telling them that many persecutions must necessarily *(dei)* be the lot of Christians in order to enter into the kingdom of God— that is, that the same pattern of suffering and glory exemplified in Jesus' life must be theirs as well if they are to know the full measure of the reign of God in their lives (cf. Mark 8:31–10:52; Rom 8:17; Phil 3:10–11; Col 1:24)." See his "The Acts of the Apostles" in *The Expositor's Bible Commentary,* 9:438.

33. For comments on the inbreaking and advance of the Kingdom, see *Revolution!,* 297–98. I do not believe the New Testament teaches that the Kingdom was offered by Jesus and then withdrawn when He was largely rejected by His people, a common teaching in dispensational circles, and that we are now in a "Church age" that excludes the Kingdom. For a New Testament theology that incorporates Kingdom truths throughout, see George Eldon Ladd, *A Theology of the New Testament,* rev. by D. A. Hagner (Grand Rapids: Eerdmans, 1993).

34. See Brown, *Our Hands Are Stained with Blood,* 165–73.

35. See www.fateh.org/e_editor/99/150399.htm.

36. The letter was dated June 7, 2001.

37. See immediately below, note 38, for websites providing excellent factual documentation of the conflict in Israel.

38. I believe Israel is in desperate need of the Messiah, being in large measure a worldly, secular and even atheistic nation (while religious Jews are especially hostile to the Gospel). And I believe there are many injustices in the land, and that we need to reach out to the Palestinians and to all Muslims with sensitivity, compassion and love. But a careful study of the information on websites such as www.debka.com, www.gamla.org and www.arutz.org will make plain where the primary culpability is found.

39. *The Christian Revolutionary,* 14, citing John A. T. Robinson, "Not Radical Enough?" *The Christian Century,* LXXXVI (Nov. 12, 1969), 1446.

## Chapter 11: *Going Outside the Camp*

1. This should not be taken as a rejection on my part of the house church movement. Rather, it is a caution against overreaction and a warning not to throw the baby out with the bath water. I would recommend some of the works cited earlier in this book, including Wolfgang Simson's *Houses That Change the World,* William Beckham's *The Second Reformation* and, more radical still, Frank Viola's *Rethinking the Wineskins.* Other relevant studies can be found in the bibliography.

2. I say "seemed to have history on its side" because, in reality, the new and better way had its origin and roots in the words of Moses and the prophets. It was the traditional religion that was actually more recent, despite its claims to go back to Moses.

3. I also find it remarkable that the religious leaders now take up the accusation that the man was blind because of his sin, the very notion refuted by Jesus at the beginning of the chapter. Note also how the story ends: The man who was blind now sees, while the religious leaders, who claimed to see, were declared blind (9:39–41).

4. *Who Is Your Covering?*, 15.

5. Don Clasen, *Submission to Spiritual Authority: A Definitive Treatment of a Modern Day Controversy*, 10, gives a good summary of this position in his critique: "The idea is that standing in submission to one's authority protects a person from spiritual attack from Satan. Submission guarantees protection, thus the need for a covering. The term also implies that God will not allow the enemy to get to you as long as you are standing under that authority. If you get out from under, you become vulnerable to anything from deception to sinful activity."

6. If this is not the case, and if instead you alone are right and no one can teach you and there is no one to whom you can submit, I have a word for you: Repent and grow up!

7. Søren Kierkegaard, *Provocations: Spiritual Writings of Kierkegaard*, compiled and edited by Charles E. Moore (Farmington, Pa.: Plough, 1999), 206–7.

8. For a small but representative sampling, see Matthew 5:10–12; 10:16–37; 16:24–25; John 12:24–25; 15:18–21; 16:1–2; 21:18–19; Acts 5:41; Romans 8:17; Philippians 1:20–21, 29; 2 Timothy 2:3; 3:12; Revelation 2:10.

9. Known around the world as "God's Smuggler"; for a short biographical study, see Brother Andrew and John and Elizabeth Sherrill, *God's Smuggler*, 35th anniversary edition (Grand Rapids: Chosen, 2001).

10. See Brown, *Revolution!*

11. Kierkegaard, *Provocations*, 205.

12. http://www.cnn.com/2000/ASIANOW/east/08/25/china.religion/index.html; August 26, 2000

13. John Howard Yoder, *The Politics of Jesus*, 2nd ed. (Grand Rapids: Eerdmans; Carlisle, U.K.: Paternoster, 1994), 33.

# Index

229

Weder, Hans, 213n.10
Wesley, Charles, 223n.20
Wesley, John, 62, 141–42, 147–48,
    182, 212.n18, 223n.20
Wesley, Samuel, 147–48
Whitefield, George, 141–42, 156,
    223n.20
Whittle, D. W., 140

Williams, Roger, 141–42, 149–51
worship, 39
"worship centers," 40
Wuest, Kenneth, 176
Wycliffe, John, 50, 210n.3(2)

Yoder, John Howard, 183, 202

**Michael L. Brown,** B.A. (Queens College), M.A. (New York University), Ph.D. (New York University), is the founder and president of the FIRE School of Ministry in Pensacola, Florida, and was the founder and past president of the Brownsville Revival School of Ministry. (FIRE is the acronym for the Fellowship for International Revival and Evangelism.) Dr. Brown has preached around the world and written more than fifteen books on revival, holiness, radical discipleship and Jewish apologetics, along with scholarly works in Old Testament and Hebrew studies.

His most recent books include *Revolution! The Call to Holy War; The Revival Answer Book: Rightly Discerning the Contemporary Revival Movements;* and *Answering Jewish Objections to Jesus* (3 volumes). He is presently working on a commentary on the book of Jeremiah for the new edition of the *Expositor's Bible Commentary.* His scholarly articles have been published in leading journals as well as in the *Oxford Dictionary of Jewish Religion, The Theological Dictionary of the Old Testament, The New International Dictionary of Old Testament Theology and Exegesis.*

He has devoted his life to helping raise up and equip an army of holy radicals who will spark a spiritual and moral revolution in this generation.

You may contact the author through

ICN Ministries
P.O. Box 36308
Pensacola, FL 32516
(850) 458-6424 phone
(850) 453-1108 fax
www.icnministries.org
www.fire-school.org